LOST IN HISTORY
1984 RECONSTRUCTED

GUNISHA KAUR

gunisha @ cornell.edu

ISBN 0-9762682-0-5

Published by:
Sikh Youth Federation
6863 Cloister Road
Toledo, OH 43617
Ph: (419) 841-7178
email: sikhs@accesstoledo.com
website: sikhyouthfederation.org

This book is dedicated to the thousands of courageous men and women across the world who have given their lives in defending the truth; who have died for our right to breathe freedom.

This book is also dedicated to my father, Satpal Singh, for his brilliant guidance, endless dedication and unconditional patience. Without his constant encouragement and motivation, this book would not have been possible.

Sources

This book is based on views and accounts from:

Amnesty International
Human-Rights Watch Asia
Physicians for Human Rights
The People's Union for Democratic Rights
The People's Union for Civil Liberties
The Citizens for Democracy
Punjab Human Rights Organization *(U.K. Branch)*
The Committee for Coordination on Disappearances in Punjab
Human Rights Wing, *Akali Dal*

United States Congressional Records
The Supreme Court of India
The Punjab and Haryana High Court

The New York Times
The Washington Post
The Economist
The New Yorker Magazine
The Christian Science Monitor
The Manchester Guardian
India Today
Baat Cheet, *Indian Army Bulletin*

Kofi Annan, *United Nations Secretary-General*
Giani Zail Singh, *former President of India*
Justice S. M. Sikri, *former Chief Justice, Supreme Court of India*
Justice V. R. Krishna Iyer, *former Justice, Supreme Court of India*

Justice V.M. Tarkunde, *former Justice, Bombay High Court*
Justice Ajit Singh Bains, *former Justice, Punjab and Haryana High Court*
HS Mattewal, *former Advocate-General, Punjab*
George Fernandes, *former Defense Minister, India*
Tapan Bose Secretary-General, *South Asia Forum for Human Rights*
Soli J. Sorabjee, *former Attorney General of India*
Eyewitnesses to the events described
Police officers and Indian Government officials

The following writers, journalists and human rights activists:

Dr. Cynthia Mahmood, *Professor, University of Notre Dame*
Dr. I. J. Singh, *Professor, New York University*
Dr. Amitav Gosh, *Distinguished Professor, Queens College, NY*
Dr. Ranbir Singh Sandhu, *retired Professor, Ohio State University, Columbus*
George Sieberer
Mary Anne Weaver
Joyce Pettigrew
Gobind Thukral
Tapash Chakraborty
Kuldip Nayar
Ram Narayan Kumar

Contents

Despite public proclamations as to the democratic nature of the Indian state and its commitments to protect human rights, the Indian Government's treatment not only of the Sikh population of Punjab but of human rights workers attempting to investigate abuses undermines its credibility. A human tragedy on the probable scale of many of the great tragedies of history has occurred in Punjab, and we do a severe disservice to those who have suffered and to those who yet may suffer when we ignore evidence to the effect that all is not well in India...

Ram Narayan Kumar (CCDP) and
Cynthia Mahmood (University of Notre Dame)[1]

When the history of Human Rights in India of our half-century comes to be written the most blood-stained pages will be reserved for the three deadly November days in the life of the nation... Where is law? Where is justice? What is the truth? Lying dead in the streets of Delhi's democracy? Where are the guilty? Untouchable and unapproachable in high offices? How can the highest in the executive and members of the Supreme Court ever command when mass casualty of human lives and rights remain a poignant interrogation?

Justice V. R. Krishna Iyer
Former Justice, Supreme Court of India[2]

Acknowledgements

Of the many people who have stood by my side in my effort to write this book, here I shall name only a few. I would like to thank Ms. Carol Palm, in whose class this project on human rights began as a 30 page paper, and who has always been the most excited to hear about my progress. I also thank Rubin Paul Singh, who provided me the initial inspiration to research the genocide of 1984. I am ever grateful and indebted to Kuldeep Singh Uncle for pushing me to make this book a reality, and Amarjit Singh Uncle, Rajinder Singh Uncle and Daljeet Singh Uncle for their guidance throughout every endeavor I have risked taking; thank you all for raising me like your daughter and giving me all the support you have been capable of giving. Thanks to Dr. I. J. Singh for his thorough input, thought provoking suggestions and as always, interesting discussions; and Navtej Singh, who has always been my favorite resource for scintillating conversation on any topic related to 1984, for his much needed advice. I am thankful to Dr. Diane Christian for her helpful suggestions that have greatly enhanced the book, Rupinder Kaur, who could never believe how much her encouragement has meant to me, as well as Kirpal Singh Nijher Uncle for his suggestions and guidance throughout the life-span of my writing. I extend a relieved thanks to Maanik Singh for preventing this book from becoming a visual disaster by preparing the cover. Further, I would like to thank Prabhjot Singh and the Sikh Coalition for their encouragement and help. A special thanks to Ishnan Kaur, of the Ontario Ministry of Education, without whom this project really could not have been completed – thank you for your patience, guidance and commitment in the production of this book.

As they say, behind every writer is an encouraging family…and friends…and family who become friends, and friends who become family. A special thanks to my mom, Narinder Kaur, who warmed my milk and cooked me food during the most intense phases of my writing; my baby brother Harmann Preet Singh who worked endlessly to match this book with one of his own; and Amandeep Singh, who has provided me more support and friendship than any sister can wish for. I would like to thank Mandeep Singh Veerji for his endless suggestions, Inderpreet Singh Veerji for his guidance and for always allowing me to tap into his vast knowledge base, Jaipal Singh for his invaluable editing and encouragement, and of course, John Paul Singh for forcing me to get involved during my year in New York City. A further thanks to my friends at NYU and Cornell who have supported me so much throughout the creation of this project. You have all been my backbone and confidence throughout these years, and I'll never forget your ever-readiness to lend a helping hand.

My deepest gratitude is due to my dad, Satpal Singh, who enthusiastically read draft after draft of this book, from its two paragraph beginnings to the finished product. He has been my inspiration for wanting to establish a greater sense of truth on the issue of human rights; he has stood by my side while I struggled with the frustration of the obstacles that prevented me from publishing this over three years ago. He has been my mentor, my confidence and my lighthouse. Thank you, Dad, for guiding this book.

Foreword

2004 marks the 20th anniversary of the tragic attacks on the Harmandir Sahib, the most significant historical Sikh Gurduara. This attack was planned thirty months before the Indian Army actually struck, according to the Commanding officer of the Western Command, Lt. General S. K. Sinha. The excuse given for this attack was to flush out a handful of alleged criminals. Similarly, in November of 1984, the pogroms against the Sikhs were also planned well ahead of time, before they actually happened in Delhi and other parts of India. Prime Minister Indira Gandhi's assassination was used as the pretext for these organized 'riots'.

In a recent article, "India's Sikhs: Waiting for Justice," published in World Policy Journal, Barbara Crossette, a renowned scholar-journalist, who was the New York Times Bureau Chief in New Delhi (1988-1991) observes: "This November will mark 20 years since those days of terror and death. Several reports by Indian human rights groups on the killings and more than half a dozen official government commissions have come, and mostly gone. Yet no Indian politician accused of complicity in fomenting the attacks has been tried. No one in authority responsible for the astonishing negligence in law enforcement has resigned." She further says, "Sikhs (as well as Muslims) will want more, however. They want justice and reparations for abuses that were encouraged, if not condoned, by politicians that have left thousands dead over two decades."

It is sad that so little has been written about the historic events that unfolded in Punjab twenty years ago. Our silence over the years has not only permitted human rights violations to persist in Punjab, but has allowed many facts to be lost in history. As a consequence of our failure to document an accurate historical account of these events, many reports now present a much distorted view of what happened in these months. In this book, Gunisha Kaur sheds light on the following important questions that come to the minds of rational people who either have witnessed this sad episode first hand or have heard about it:

1. How was it possible for a country that claims to be secular in character, non-violent and democratic, to carry out a massacre of its own people for no reason other than that they were Sikhs?
2. How was it possible for the Sikh Nation to allow almost their entire younger generation to be destroyed by such violence?
3. How was it possible for the world to stand by without halting the destruction?

Gunisha Kaur is one of those rare individuals who has spoken up amidst the silence. Four years ago, she was inspired after attending a workshop on the 1984 genocide at a Sikh Youth Federation camp and immediately began researching the subject. By writing this book, she has brought to the attention of the world just one chapter out of a series of chapters that need to be written to describe the mentality of the ruling elite in India. She is the first youth scholar, inspired by the knowledge she obtained from the Sikh Youth Federation camp as well as other Sikh institutions, who has presented the facts of history in the language of American born youth by putting her heart and soul into this project.

Toledo, October 20, 2004   Kuldeep Singh
President, Sikh Youth Federation
Chairman, World Sikh Council (America Region)

Preface

Four years ago saw the birth of this project on human rights. The motivation for this book came from the desire to publish an unbiased version of the 1984 siege and attack of a great Sikh gurduara, the Harmandir Sahib. Over the years, I have tried my hardest to conduct a thorough and unbiased search into the nature of the attack. Though the facts established by reputable authorities are not biased, I cannot say the same for my emotions. This project is by no means flawless, and though a strong attempt was made, it may not be perfectly unbiased. It is a collection of facts, emotions and reflections on the situation in India since her independence from British rule.

One of my favorite writers once told me that we will always look back at our writing and wonder how we ever wrote the way we did – there will always be improvements that can be made, and we could spend our entire lives editing. The situation here is as such. Yet there comes a point where we should edit no more – where the necessity and importance of presenting the information that we have is overbearing – where we must present our work just the way it is. Please excuse the many imperfections in this book, because though improvements can be made forever, the hour has come that necessitates the presentation of these facts in just the form that they are in.

Though this work may be emotionally biased, it is surely not biased in evidence. A great deal of the information here has been provided by human rights agencies such as Amnesty International, Human Rights Watch, and the United Nations. The most shocking bits of evidence

have come from highly respected authorities from within and outside
of India, such as former Prime Ministers of India, Justices and Chief
Justices of the High Courts and Supreme Court of India, as well as
U.S. Congressmen. The remaining testimonies and accounts come
from local Punjabis – any bias that exists stems mainly from the pain
in their poignant stories.

It has become a tendency of supporters of the Indian government,
Indira Gandhi, or Operation Bluestar to blame the occurrences in
1984 on Baba Jarnail Singh Bhindranwale. Even more frequently, people who believe that he was an extremist or do not concur with his
views on Sikhism blame the invasion on his presence in the Akal
Takht. This book does not serve as a testimony to any view of Baba
Jarnail Singh Bhindranwale. It diffracts the question of his presence in
the Akal Takht for a more pressing one. When I printed the first copy
of this book in my junior year of high school, an acquaintance of
mine suggested that she knew eleven and a half reasons as to why
Operation Bluestar was justified. How can eleven and a half reasons
justify the slaughter of tens of thousands of *innocents*? This is my question to the people that believe that Baba Jarnail Singh Bhindranwale
was the reason that the Indian Army razed the Akal Takht and the
Harmandir Sahib and killed thousands and thousands of innocent
Sikhs after the buildings were in the army's control.

The reaction of this acquaintance to my book is a common one. Most
people interpret the Indian government's abuse of the Sikh population

as friction between the Hindus and the Sikhs. This blanket statement could not be more inaccurate. The tension that existed was between the Hindu-dominated Indian government and the Sikhs, not between the Hindus and the Sikhs. This distinction is very precarious, for even a slight slip can cause bitter hatred and division. The criticism of fanatic Hindu organizations and a fanatic Hindu government hardly implies criticism of the entire group of religious followers. So many of these people have risked their own lives and the survival of their families to save their Sikh brothers. When my own father was trapped near Bhopal during the pogroms in November of 1984, his life was saved several times through the intervention of Hindus he did not even know. In large part, the few Sikhs that survived the government's machinations owe their lives to their Hindu neighbors.

My eyes have run dry, and there are no tears left to shed, after looking at the pictures of tortured children and molested women, and reading the grotesque stories of brutalized Sikh men. Sadly, the facts presented in this book represent only a small fraction of the human rights violations that are occurring throughout the world even today. Sitting in the comfort of our homes, it is easy to bestow the responsibility of taking action on others. I cannot emphasize enough how vital it is that everyone speak out against human rights violations that are occurring, for the common cliché could not be more true: there is power in numbers. Through media, books, articles or letters to congress – it is imperative that each and every one of us fulfills our responsibility to humanity.

The genocide in 1984 and subsequent events are being lost in history, buried under governmental politics, international relations and sheer silencing of human rights workers. On this 20th anniversary of the Sikh holocaust, it has been my goal to recover and dust off the hidden atrocities that have occurred and are still occurring in Punjab today. It is not my goal to convince anyone of anything that I believe, but simply to provide the facts and allow the reader to make an *educated* decision, rather than one based on prejudice or emotions. From here it is the reader's prerogative to research more and take action against human rights violations. The contribution of each person, no matter how small, is still significant, and is the only means to free the world of the mass religious and ethnic cleansings that continue unabated until this day, whether it is in India, Rwanda or Darfur.

Gunisha Kaur
September 22, 2004

CHAPTER 1
The Genesis of Genocide

...a just society cannot be built on tolerance for the most egregious acts of violence that occurred in the past, and... a society cannot heal and achieve new levels of unity and solidarity by turning away from the plight of those who suffered, and are still suffering.

Kofi Annan, United Nations Secretary General[3]

Murder. No, not murder. Genocide. The cruel and inhumane torture and killing of tens of thousands of religious devotees from June 3rd to June 6th, 1984, can only be referred to as government planned genocide. The national army with one instruction and the fascist government with one goal: suffocation of the entire religion. To this day the horrific events that took place in Amritsar, India, only twenty years ago, remain unknown to most of the world.

Why would any government plot the execution of an entire religious group? To find this answer we must take a close look at the political situation in India at the time, and the determination of the Sikh people to fight the government's blatant oppression of its citizens.

Born into a tradition of religious fervor and military zeal, Sikhs are well known for their role as saint-soldiers. To a devout Sikh, piousness and the defense of the defenseless are equally important aspects of Sikhism; thus in addition to adhering to their religious principles, the Sikhs were to stand up for what they believed in, and protect those

1

who could not stand up for themselves. They were to protect not only other Sikhs, but anyone who fell victim to tyranny and injustice.

From the very inception of the religion, Sikhs have been at the forefront of battles and wars, for the common stereotype is true – the Sikhs are great warriors. Yet this definition of warrior does not convey the empty and ruthless murder with which we so readily equate it today. This definition of warrior is wholly exclusive of the drive to kill, for the Sikhs have always been the upholders of justice and peace. Through their own history, they have fought only when all peaceful measures have failed, with almost all of their battles being defensive rather than offensive. The Sikhs are great warriors, not great killers.

Nor are they a violent people. Rather, the Sikhs have fought with necessity, and have always been the hand of justice.

Each of the ten Sikh Gurus emphasized the message of peace, equality, and universal brotherhood in a society where the caste system prevailed. A little over three centuries ago, Guru Gobind Singh, the 10th Guru of the Sikhs, gave them a lofty code of conduct and a distinct identity, which included the maintenance of unshorn hair and a kirpan[4], which symbolized the protection of the suppressed.

By virtue of their outspoken stand against oppression, the Sikhs presented a grave danger to the tyrannical Indian government. Indira Gandhi, the Prime Minister at the time, realized this threat. In 1975, Indira Gandhi had been convicted of election fraud by the Uttar Pradesh High Court, which ordered her to be removed as the Prime Minister of India. Yet by declaring a National Emergency and suspending the Indian constitution with all its guarantees, she retained her power, imposing a dictatorial rule in India from 1975 until 1977. The Sikhs strongly opposed this oppressive control, and over 50,000 courted arrest by peacefully marching out of the Harmandir Sahib (also known as the Darbar Sahib or the Golden Temple), while singing religious hymns.[5] When India went to elections in 1977, Indira Gandhi lost by a landslide. When she came back to power in 1980, she was not only angry about her earlier loss of power, but was also bitter towards the Sikhs for having opposed her –

during the National Emergency. She was aware that as they had done in the past, the Sikhs would surely oppose any tyrannical measures that she would take. In her eyes, there was only one solution to the problem: she would crush the Sikhs' spirit and destroy their valor, so that they would never again rise in the face of oppression.

However, since human rights organizations such as Amnesty International were already wary of the grave injustices taking place in India, Ms. Gandhi needed a valid excuse and a deceptive plot to eradicate her enemy. The very successful Sikh agitation demanding decentralization of political power and acknowledgement of Sikh grievances provided Indira Gandhi with such an excuse. The plot consisted of destroying the heart of the Sikh spirit and power, the Harmandir Sahib and the Akal Takhat, and eliminating its very charismatic spiritual leader, Baba Jarnail Singh Bhindranwale.

On June 3rd, 1984, the Indian government launched a full-scale assault on the Harmandir Sahib, claiming that they needed to eliminate Jarnail Singh and other alleged terrorists from the inside of the complex. As Operation Bluestar was set in motion, the premeditated slaughter of tens of thousands of innocent pilgrims commenced.

Subsequent to this attack on the Harmandir Sahib, several hundreds of thousands of Sikhs have been killed or tortured to death under different pretexts. One picture, provided by the villagers of Shutrana, shows the brutal police torture of Avtar Singh. The innocent man is shown with his limbs disjointed, patches of his skin burnt away by the use of an iron and large areas of his bone exposed by the use of electrodes. Hot rods were used to pierce the soles of his feet, and his flesh was pulled with pliers.[6] This example is cited here not because of the harsh uniqueness of the case, but rather, to exemplify a routine way of torturing and killing Sikhs in India. Just as the Jews were killed in the Holocaust for the simple reason that they were Jews, the Sikhs were butchered in India for the simple reason that they were Sikhs. Anyone who looks like a Sikh may be branded as a terrorist and taken to an interrogation center (a euphemism for a torture chamber), never to be seen or heard from again. As Dr. I.J. Singh so eloquently states, "There was no trial and no justice."[7]

3

Independent non-Sikh human rights organizations such as Amnesty International have been branded as "terrorist sympathizers"[8] by the Indian government for their efforts to bring justice to the victims and their families, and have not been allowed inside parts of Punjab to investigate the odious crimes against humanity.[9] Several books that address the topic of the Sikh Holocaust have been banned by the Indian government and have been labeled as seditious, even though they have been written and published by highly respected non-Sikh organizations. The few copies of these books that *were* available were confiscated or burnt shortly thereafter, allowing the government officials and politicians to escape any form of criticism or scrutiny. Those that *do* know the truth about Operation Bluestar cannot tell their stories, for they have been silenced by man's worst enemy: fear. They fear for their lives and for the lives of their children, for revealing the truth about the holocaust that was so carefully and maliciously covered-up by the Indian government means certain death. Thus the poignant reality of the human rights violations in India remains solely in the hearts of those who have miraculously survived the wrath of their own government; their extraordinary stories will be sealed by their deaths.

The Citizens for Democracy is one of the most prestigious human rights organizations in India. Comprised of a retired Supreme Court Justice and five other eminent Indian citizens (only one of whom is a Sikh), this fact-finding team served as one of the most impartial and unbiased investigators into the crimes of 1984 and the subsequent atrocities. In their report to the nation, *Oppression In Punjab*, which was banned by the government, the group sheds light on the situation in India[10]:

> *Today, it is the State itself which openly indulges not only in murder and assault, but also in inhumane torture, molestation of women, non-production of the accused before a Magistrate, destruction of crops, frequent raids, and harassment of the friends and relatives of the accused and false encounters leading to gruesome deaths.*

This is the condition of the world's largest democracy, which the United Nations itself lauds for its dedication to the protection of the rights of minorities.[11] Faced with such lucid and undeniable evidence of the grave human rights violations that are occurring in India even at this moment, how can we, with a clear conscience, turn a blind eye to the plight of hundreds of thousands of innocent men, women, and children that continue to suffer at the hands of their oppressive government? Dr. I. J. Singh from New York University also comments on the present situation of Sikhs in India in his essay *1984 Revisited*[12]:

> *If I can discuss apartheid in South Africa why not the genocidal policies of an Indian government against its own people...there is no guarantee that evidence will last, nor that it will not be tarnished in time. If some objectivity can come with time, so can hardened prejudice. There is no reason for neglect. Years from now historians will reconstruct history from what we have said today...Respectable authors like Patwant Singh and Khushwant Singh, who have no truck with Sikh separatists, have labeled the killings of Sikhs in India government inspired and organized, akin to the Nazi pogroms against the Jews. Tell the Jews worldwide that what happened to them in Nazi Germany is of no concern outside the borders of Germany. Tell the world that what happens in the Middle East today is irrelevant to the Jew or Arab living in America.*

Many of our nation's leaders who are dedicated to the ideals of democracy have brought the issue of the injustices against minorities in India to the House and Senate floors. Over one hundred congressmen wrote to President Ronald Reagan demanding action against India for her crimes in 1984. On February 28th, 2002, forty-two congressmen appealed to President George W. Bush for the release of over 50,000 political Sikh prisoners that are being held illegally in

Indian jails even today. We must follow in their path and petition for recognition of what India has done to her people by the United States and other governments. Only by taking a stand can we demonstrate to the Indian government that what they have done will not be tolerated, and hope to avoid such atrocities in the future. By ignoring the human rights violations that are taking place, we are acquiescing to the tyranny and injustice – how can we both call ourselves a democratic nation, and silently condone torture, rape, and genocide? We have become, sadly, no better than the oppressor itself.

Yet among this mountain of fear, oppression, brutality and the nadir of human nature, one element stands tall and proud: the valor and spirit of a brave people, who have the courage to die so that others can live and breathe in freedom. This is the untold story of those great martyrs.

CHAPTER 2
Broken Promises

I ask you [Sikhs] to accept my word...and the resolution of the Congress that it will not betray a single individual, much less a community...our Sikh friends have no reason to fear that it would betray them. For, the moment it does so, the Congress would not only thereby seal its own doom but that of the country too. Moreover, Sikhs are a brave people. They know how to safeguard their rights by exercise of arms if it should ever come to that.

Mohandas Gandhi[13]

Since before India's independence in 1947, the Sikhs had been recognized by national leaders for their staunch participation in all Indian affairs. Although they were numerically in a great minority, the Sikhs had contributed more arms and men than all other citizens combined for the independence of their homeland. Leading the army in India's wars against the British as well as the Chinese, the Sikhs had zealously served their country.[14]

In return for their patriotic services, the Sikhs were guaranteed fulfillment of their only desire – freedom to practice their religion in peace. As India gained independence however, the promises that had been so keenly made by the Congress leaders to the Sikhs, were broken one by one.

In the early 1900s, India sought to gain freedom from the British Raj that had controlled her for more than a hundred years. The Sikhs led the way with their heroic displays of courage as the Indian Army defended its homeland. They were given recognition from both the British and the Indians for their crucial role in the struggle for freedom. As both sides were well aware, without the Sikhs, independence from British rule would be nearly impossible.

Over the course of the struggle for independence, several propositions were made to the Sikhs in order to get them to break their loyalty to the Congress of India. At the time of the Second Round Table Conference in 1932, the British government informally made a proposal to the Sikhs: if they dissociated themselves from the movement for independence, they would be given complete sovereign control of Punjab, their homeland. Although they refused this offer and continued fighting for India's independence, a second confidential proposal was made by influential members of the British Cabinet to the Sikh representative Baldev Singh, under which the Sikhs would be given a political status that would permit them "to have political feet of their own on which they may walk into the current of world history."[15] After little thought and consideration however, he informed the British government that the Sikhs intended to have their political aspirations fulfilled by the majority community, and that the Congress Party had already promised Master Tara Singh and Baldev Singh that the Sikhs would have a prominent role in the functioning of the Indian government. Thus instead of gaining their own independent homeland, Punjab, by simply leaving the independence movement, they remained loyal to India and the Congress.

The sacrifices of the fervent Sikhs for their country, in the struggle for freedom from the British, are displayed in the table below[16]:

Punishment/Participation	Sikhs	Non-Sikhs	Total	% Sikhs
Died	1,557	618	2,175	71 %
Imprisoned For Life	2,147	499	2,646	81 %
Killed at Jallianwala Bagh	799	501	1,300	61 %
Indian National Army	20,000	12,000	32,000	63 %

Although they made up only 2% of the Indian population at the time, 71% of the people that died fighting for India's independence were Sikhs. Prime Minister Jawahar Lal Nehru acknowledged the Sikhs' sacrifices at the all-India committee meeting in Calcutta in 1946 when he stated, "...the brave Sikhs of Punjab are entitled to special consideration. I see nothing wrong in an area and a set-up in the North wherein the Sikhs can also experience the glow of freedom."[17] Later, with the formal promises of a religious homeland, the Sikhs fought with the impression that they would not only gain independence for their motherland, India, but also gain the freedom to express their religious beliefs in peace.

On August 15th, 1947, India celebrated its independence from British rule. This same day however, the homeland of the Sikhs was carved up between Pakistan and India, leaving only the east side to the community that had so passionately defended the country. Contrary to all of their hopes and dreams, the Sikhs were driven out of their homes on the west side (which held 78% of the fertile and irrigated lands) due to this division, and were left as poor orphans without any aid from India. Nearly 40% of the Sikh population was forced to abandon their homes, with another 2.5% being brutally massacred. Yet the Sikhs bravely left Pakistan to fulfill their new dreams of prosperity and happiness in a now divided Punjab.[18]

The first sign of the fate of those dreams came in the form of a memo, unknown to most of the Sikhs even today. While on one hand the Congress and police officials stated that the Sikhs, as national heroes, had been deprived of valuable lives and great wealth, on the other hand a confidential memo sent by the government to all of the Deputy Commissioners on October 10th, 1947 stated[19]:

The Sikhs, as a community, were a lawless people and were thus a menace to the law abiding Hindus in the province. The Deputy Commissioners are hereby called upon to take special measures against them. You are also instructed that no Sikh will cross Ambala. Keep these germs and bacteria contained between Wagah border and Ambala.

Within the next few years, the Congress had the difficult and trying task of creating a national constitution. As they had been promised by several government officials, the Sikhs expected to exert control over their homeland, Punjab, with minimal ties to the Indian government. Yet with each new year that passed, the Sikhs became more and more aware that the only thing that had been assured to them were empty promises. In 1950, the Congress affirmed this suspicion by declaring their intention of having a strongly centralized government. Although the Sikhs vehemently protested, their voices were not heard. Punjab was going to be largely run by the centralized government, with the Sikhs wielding the least amount of control possible. Additionally, it would become a bilingual state, housing both Punjabi and Hindi, regardless of the fact that only the former was spoken in Punjab. As David Crystal said[20]:

> *Language is more than a shared code of symbols for communication. People do not fight and die, as they have done in India, to preserve a set of symbols. They do so because they feel that their identity is at stake – that language preservation is a question of human rights, community status and nationhood.*

Out of the fourteen languages recognized by the Constitution of India, Punjabi was the only one not granted a state on its basis. The promises made to the people who contributed the most to the freedom of the country were forgotten as India became a sovereign republic with its own constitution. The politicians and leaders of the time felt that any demand for language preservation or a language based state meant that the Sikhs were demanding a separate identity.

As Dr. Ranbir Singh Sandhu says in his book *Struggle for Justice*, "Many Hindus hold the description of the Sikh faith being distinct from Hindu as a mark of hostility."[21] In *Tragedy of Punjab*[22], Kuldip Nayar and Khushwant Singh further describe how the Hindus were hurt by the statement made by Akalis to the effect that the Sikhs were a separate nation. Despite the fact that the two religions share virtually nothing in common (e.g., Sikhism is monotheistic while Hinduism is pantheistic), the government continues to make an unabated effort even today to dilute the identity of Sikhs and incorporate them into the majority religion. Inderjit Singh Jaijee comments on the impossibility of surviving as a minority religion in India when he states[23]:

Religions which lacked any "support base" outside the country were soon assimilated into the amorphous matrix of Hinduism. This is what happened to the Indian Buddhists in the early centuries of this millennium. It happened to the Jains and the Lingayats as well. After independence the various indigenous religio-cultural tribal groups felt the tendrils of Hinduism tighten around them.

The constitution of India does not even recognize Sikhism as a distinct religion. It considers Sikhism a sect of Hinduism, which is akin to calling Christianity a sect of Hinduism. The promise that the constitution would not be drafted and implemented without the Sikhs' consent had been blatantly broken, as had Prime Minister Nehru's promise that the Punjabi culture and language would be preserved. Hukam Singh and Bhupinder Singh Mann, the representatives of the Sikh community to the Constituent Assembly, therefore did not sign the constitution. When Prime Minister Nehru was reminded of the promises that he had personally made to the Sikhs, he stated, "The Sikhs have missed the bus."[24]

The Congress had successfully destroyed the Sikh homeland economically with the partitioning of Punjab, and had succeeded in hindering the perpetuation of the Punjabi language. It was evident that the Congress aimed to slowly eradicate the Sikhs' culture and religion, which they felt was a threat to their own power and glory.

The troubles had only begun however, as the Chinese invaded the Indian border in 1962. Once again, the Sikhs were needed to give up their lives for a country that thought them too ignoble to even recognize their religion or their language. Yet they fought. Three years later, in 1965, the war with Pakistan began. The situation became so desperate for India that the senior army officials decided to give up almost 1/3 of Punjab and retreat to a point beyond the river Beas. Yet the Sikh General, Harbakhash Singh, and his army refused to yield any part of the country. With a fierce battle against immensely heavy odds, they repulsed Pakistani attacks and actually drove the enemy behind their own line of defense (to the Ichhogil Canal). More passionately than they had in the war for independence and contributing more material and men to the army than all of the other states in India combined, the Sikhs defended their homeland once again. Although the government tried for a second time to rebuff the astounding role that the Sikhs had played, the public felt that a Punjabi-speaking state was both appropriate and necessary. Thus in 1966, the linguistic reorganization of Punjab was granted.[25]

As it finally seemed that events were taking an upward turn, the government found yet another way to impede the progress of the Sikhs. Spearheaded by Indira Gandhi and G. L. Nanda, the Punjab Reorganization Act of 1966 had a two-fold impact: First, it gave control of the pivotal river waters in agriculture-based Punjab to the centralized Indian government, who proceeded to strip the Sikhs of their water-rights. Secondly, it dissected Punjab into four parts, donating the most important and vital areas to neighboring states.[26] Not only did the Congress deprive the Sikhs of the land and water that they had been promised for decades, it stripped away Punjab's economic potential by doing so. With almost all of the water resources and strategically located cities being redistricted into other areas, the state and its people had been denied any prospect of prospering by the same country that they had given their flesh and blood in defending.

After contributing more than any other group to India's independence from the British and the wars against China and Pakistan, the Sikhs were only rewarded with hatred and inequality. With the grossly discriminatory anti-Sikh Congress in the ruling, the foundations for political unrest and dissatisfaction had been laid.

CHAPTER 3
The Building of Tensions

The American Supreme Court ruled, in the infamous Skokie case, that the Constitution's First Amendment protected even the neo-Nazi's right to march through an area of Holocaust survivors in Illinois carrying swastikas. Here in the largest democracy of the world, we are not even allowed to hear complaints of heinous human rights crimes from the people whom the State has decreed to disappear in total obscurity. A State that deems the victims of human rights crimes to be too ignoble even to be heard should at least stop pretending that it respects their citizenship.

Committee for Coordination on Disappearances in Punjab[27]

After eighteen years of struggle for a homeland, the Sikhs were granted a dissected and repartitioned Punjab. As a result of the divisions that were surfacing within the Akali Dal[28] in 1960, however, two factions of the party had been created: one led by Master Tara Singh, the legendary hero of the War of Independence, and one led by Baba Fateh Singh, the President of the Shiromani Akali Dal. Without one single strong leader or political party, the Sikhs were never able to form their own pure government. The power fell into the hands of those who had corrupted India to begin with. Though this speaks poorly of the Sikhs' ability to form a united government under their political wing even in an area where they were undeniably in a majority, the fact remains that the government of Punjab was controlled largely by those very leaders that the Sikhs had denounced in the central government.

The Nirankari Jatha[29] is a religious group that is strongly associated with Arya Samaj[30] and other such organizations that are borne from the desire to reform old age Hinduism. A specific sect of the Nirankaris, called the Nakli Nirankaris by many, aimed not at the reformation of the common Hindu man, but at promoting a distorted version of Sikhism. Arya Samaj and the Nakli Nirankaris led by Gurbachan Singh, aimed to destroy the individuality and uniqueness of Sikhism and incorporate it into Hinduism. Although it is portrayed as though these groups are acting independently to mislead the Sikh religion, it is a strongly held belief by many Sikhs that these organizations are backed by the Indian government.

In 1978, the Nirankaris decided to organize a convention in Amritsar on April 13th, one of the holiest days for the Sikhs.[31] One day prior to the convention however, they hosted a procession in which their leader, Gurbachan Singh, made several offensive comments about the Sikh religion. Hurt by his abusive words, one hundred members of the Akhand Kirtani Jatha[32] and Damdami Taksal marched to the convention the next day to peacefully demonstrate their dissatisfaction towards the derogatory comments. Equipped with rifles and stenguns, the Nirankaris opened fire on the peacefully protesting Sikhs, killing thirteen and wounding seventy-eight. Adding further enormity to the situation, the police, instead of protecting the defenseless Sikhs, threw tear gas at them.[33]

The Sikhs, greatly disturbed by this random act of violence, requested that those responsible for these intolerable acts be punished in accordance with the law. Additionally, they wanted assurance that no one would desecrate the sanctity of the Guru Granth Sahib, the Sikh equivalent of the Christian Bible or the Muslim Qur'an. Considering the pattern of discrimination on the basis of religion in a country that vehemently proclaims a separation of church and state, these requests were both appropriate and necessary.

14

To subside the strong campaign by the Sikhs against this attack, the state charged the Nirankaris that were present at the time of the attack with murder, including their chief, Gurbachan Singh.[34] Yet the charges against Gurbachan Singh never reached the judge. He was bailed out of jail, with his case being transferred to Haryana. From his surprising release, it became evident that Gurbachan Singh had strong backing from influential members of the Congress. Further infuriating the Sikhs, the Nirankaris involved in the murders were released, as the judge claimed that they had acted in self-defense.[35] As Dr. Ranbir Singh Sandhu says in his book *Struggle for Justice*[36]:

> *Every attempt was made to avoid punishing the guilty. Instead of apprehending those who had committed the heinous crime, the local authorities escorted them safely out of the state.*

Over a dozen Sikhs were killed in a second Nirankari-Sikh clash that took place in 1978, but this time, by police firing. As in the prior incident, the Sikhs were peacefully protesting the insulting comments made by the Nirankaris toward their religion and their Guru.

It had become very clear to the public by this time that the freedoms that define a democracy were being limited by the Government of India, led by Indira Gandhi. Article 3 of the Indian Constitution guarantees, "the right to life, liberty and security of person." This clearly did not apply to the Sikhs that were murdered first by an anti-Sikh coalition, and then by their own government in 1978. Denial of justice in the face of a clear violation of human rights led to many more peaceful protests, and much more resentment against the tyrannical government.

In 1975, Prime Minister Indira Gandhi was found guilty of election fraud by the Uttar Pradesh High Court. In order to maintain her power however, she declared a National Emergency and suspended the Indian Constitution. The situation became extraordinarily oppressive, with people in the country completely unsure of what action to take next. The solution came in the form of a non-violent protest by the Sikhs. They campaigned against the repression by singing religious hymns while marching out of the Harmandir Sahib by the hundreds (this centuries old practice of the Sikhs had also been adopted by Mohandas Gandhi during the struggle for independence from the British). Within a matter of months, over 50,000 Sikhs were imprisoned for their campaign against the destruction of democracy. Indira Gandhi would never forget that the Sikhs had opposed her dictatorship. Whereas Mohandas Gandhi was championed for his civil disobedience campaign, the Sikhs were demonized and punished. Their peaceful marches were not only met with harsh police action, but also with an oppressive clamping down on human rights as the Sikhs sustained their protest and the National Emergency continued.

When Indira Gandhi returned to power in 1980, she dismissed the Akali government and replaced it with a Congress regime led by her toady, Darbara Singh, as the Chief Minister of Punjab.[37] Ms. Gandhi used the Nirankari-Sikh tension as an opportunity to gain political advantage in 1980. With the goal of winning the votes of the Hindu population in Northern India and Punjab, she sought to create hostility between the Hindus and the Sikhs where it had never existed before; Indira Gandhi began state sponsored terrorism against devout Sikhs. As a reaction to this unjust treatment, the Sikhs launched a non-violent counter-campaign and started publicly exposing the specific police and political leaders who were responsible for committing the persecution. As a result of these exposures, some police and political leaders fell victim to the anger of the people, reactions that the government blamed on the Sikhs. It was through creating a hostile mind-set that Indira Gandhi was able to set the stage for a hostile environment. Between 1982 and 1983, the tensions between the Hindu community and the Sikh community escalated exponentially, with the government endorsing violence, and in most cases, instigating violent acts themselves. Dr. Ranbir Singh Sandhu describes the situation in the following lines :

> *To brand devout Sikhs as criminals, the Government stage-managed numerous crimes. The police would orchestrate a crime and then ascribe it to Sant Bhindranwale. Following this, the law-enforcement agencies would round up devout Sikhs and harass, torture, rape and often 'eliminate' them.*

As the government was gaining more and more strength from anti-Sikh politicians, a religious leader, Baba Jarnail Singh Bhindranwale, launched a campaign against the Arya Samaj and other fanatic Hindu organizations that had as their missions the misleading of Sikhs. Possibly the most demonized leader of modern history, Jarnail Singh spearheaded the agitation for human rights throughout Punjab and the rest of India. Most of his following developed from the young rural Sikh population in Punjab who were greatly disappointed with the government's unequal treatment of the Punjabi people. First, the government had stripped them of their water rights, reducing the majority of farmers to poverty, and then they plagued their homeland with alcohol and other intoxicants to gain money in the form of excise taxes. These young boys were disgusted by the poverty that the new government's rule had brought to the land that their brothers had died protecting. These people were not separatists. They were not extremists, nor were they terrorists. They were poor farmers from Punjab who wanted changes to be implemented in their government, so that they too, would have the opportunity and ability to prosper like the rest of India.

The government, led by Prime Minister Indira Gandhi, sought to suppress this movement for equality while seeking further political profit from the situation. Jarnail Singh was rapidly gaining influence and power, and they needed a quick outlet to discredit his movement. Since his speeches were made almost entirely in Punjabi, the government found it quite easy to misquote and misrepresent Jarnail Singh. They began by maligning his name through the media to gain support for the anti-Sikh pogroms that were to follow. The government-sponsored news portrayed him as a violent extremist and secessionist who wanted the Sikh equivalent of the Muslim's Pakistan, named Khalistan. Yet contrary to the popular belief that most people hold even today, Jarnail Singh did not ask for a separate nation for the Sikhs. In fact, on May 11th, 1983, he explicitly stated in a speech, "How can a nation which has sacrificed so much for the freedom of the country want it fragmented?"[39] New York Times writer William Stevens stated, "...one possible explanation advanced for the Government's raising of the Khalistan question is that it needs to...justify the killings in Amritsar and the invasion of the Sikhs' holiest shrine."[40]

Indian Security Forces murdered hundreds of Sikhs between 1981 and 1984 in fake 'encounters', using the tension between the government and the Sikhs as an excuse for unbridled state power. Over 100,000 Sikhs courted arrest[41] during this period while peacefully demanding the rights that they had been promised when India had gained its independence from Britain. The Citizens for Democracy report states[42]:

> *The ruling political party set up organizations to promote divisions within the Sikh religion, encouraged insult and abuse of leaders and founders of the faith, and interfered in religious matters. To preserve their identity, the Sikhs agitated for increased state autonomy, constitutional amendment to recognize their religion as separate from Hindu, and certain territorial and river-water rights [as provided by the national law]. The government treated their peaceful protest as sedition; demand for recognition of their religion as secessionism; confirmation in their religion as separatism, wearing of the external symbols of their religion as extremism, and the bearing of arms – required for all "Amritdhari[43]" Sikhs – as terrorism and armed insurrection...*

The report further stated[44]:

> *Amritdhari Sikhs are not "dangerous criminals" as the obsessed Army has declared, but the Amritdhari Sikhs are in danger – their fate is uncertain.*

During this time, most acts of violence that occurred against Hindus were pinned on Baba Jarnail Singh in order to create a rift between the Hindu and the Sikh communities, and to ease the passage of anti-Sikh legislation.[45] As independent investigative teams have found, these acts had almost always been staged by the Indian government to further legitimize the terrorism that was about to be unleashed against the Sikhs.[46] In addition, although the crime rate in Punjab was commendably lower than the Indian national figures, the image of crime in the state was severely exaggerated in order to gain public consent for state-sponsored oppression.[47] A senior officer in Punjab's capital stated in *India Today* on December 31, 1983, "It's really shocking that we have so little against him [Jarnail Singh] while we keep blaming him for all sorts of things."[48] Yet gaining the support of the Northern Hindu population would mean certain victory for Indira Gandhi in the upcoming election of 1985. Thus, she encouraged the spreading of vicious rumors about Jarnail Singh and his followers, and allowed them to plague the minds of the trusting Indians.

At the height of the campaign against the Sikh agitation for equality in 1981, Baba Jarnail Singh was arrested for murder, which to the Sikhs showed clear intentions on the part of the government to malign his name (as he was released shortly after the arrest due to the lack of police evidence against him). In the second half of that year, Baba Jarnail Singh moved into the Harmandir Sahib Complex, and later to the Akal Takhat, which stands within the complex. In November of 1983, Indira Gandhi had herself written a letter to Baba Jarnail Singh praising his novel ideas and views on social issues.[49] Yet after his move into the Harmandir Sahib, she declared President's Rule[50] in the state of Punjab, which held a chilling reminder of the National Emergency days. According to the report *Dead Silence: The Legacy of Abuses in*

Punjab, created by Human Rights Watch Asia and Physicians for Human Rights, "The arbitrary manner in which president's rule has been invoked in Punjab and other states has led critics to observe that it has become a tool for purely partisan purposes."[51] Claiming that the country was in a state of emergency, Ms. Gandhi warned that certain laws were going to be suspended.

The campaign against Sikhism continued, with hundreds of Sikhs being butchered by their government every month. The horrifying atrocities of June 1984 were only a few months away, as Indira Gandhi and her Congress prepared for the biggest genocide and mass murder in the history of modern India.

CHAPTER 4
Oppression Bluestar

...bodies were being brought in municipal garbage trucks round the clock since early 6 June. We have been really busy. To add to our woes, we don't have enough wood to burn the dead...

Brahma Challaney, Associated Press of America
(citing the man on duty at the city's crematorium)[52]

There are few things that will bring tears to a man's eyes, and fewer still that he will admit to. Yet no man can deny the poignancy of the events that unveiled in Punjab in 1984, and of the terror in the stories told by those few Sikhs that survived the unilateral attack of the Harmandir Sahib by their own government. On June 1st, 1984, the Indian government commenced its full-scale assault on the most sacred Sikh gurduara[53], the Harmandir Sahib. As the Sikh Vatican, the Harmandir Sahib stood as the source of peaceful movements for acknowledgment of human rights as well as political decentralization in India. Though the purpose of Operation Bluestar according to the government was to weed out terrorists and recover illegal arms and ammunition from the gurduara , the Sikhs of Punjab see the aggression in a different light[55]:

"Operation Bluestar" is the Government's term, connoting a necessary military operation to flush out terrorists and recover arms from the Golden Temple; the implication being that it was an unavoidable cleansing operation, an act of purification. Whereas "Ghallughara"

21

*is how the Sikhs of Punjab remember the episode,
connoting aggression, mass-massacre and religious
persecution.*

The invasion had been planned close to thirty months prior to June 1984
by Major-General Brar and Lieutenant-General Ranjit Singh Dayal, with
the guidance of their superior officer Lieutenant-General Krishnaswamy
Sunderji.[56] Taking into consideration that the army units had been practic-
ing on a replica of the Harmandir Sahib on the interior of the Garhwal
Hills months before the invasion, it is clear that this was neither a last
minute response, nor an only resort to terrorist threats supposedly com-
ing from within the complex.[57] Additionally, something must have lead
Prime Minister Indira Gandhi to chose the date that she did. Done not
out of forgetfulness, but out of careful deliberation, the Indian government chose to attack the Harmandir Sahib on June 1st, the martyrdom
day of the fifth Guru of the Sikhs, Guru Arjan Dev. As one of the most
well attended Sikh religious holidays, it was clear that the greatest number of devotees would be inside. What ensued was a deliberate, heartless
massacre by a government of its own citizens.

The stories of the following people have been presented in the report
Oppression in Punjab by the Citizens for Democracy. This report,
which is banned in India, serves to, "tell the truth, the as-yet untold
story and in the process to correct the Government's version as put out
by the Army, the Press, the Radio, the T.V. and the White Paper."[58]
Founded by Jaya Prakasyh Narayan, a Hindu who stood as a civil
rights leader of great national prominence, the Citizens for Democracy
functions as one of the most reliable human rights organizations in
India. Although oral history has its own drawbacks, it remains an
invaluable source of knowledge for future generations. If enough witnesses are interviewed, the dissimilarities and erroneous information is
sure to be weeded out.

The similarity between the stories of the survivors of the Sikh holocaust cannot be of mere coincidence. Although they differ greatly
from the government's version as published in the *White Paper*, these

personal experiences and witnesses' accounts contain the same dates, times, and descriptions of events, proving to be nothing but the whole truth. To avoid redundancy, presented here will be the story of only a few survivors. To see the remarkable similarities between all of the stories, it is worthwhile to read Part II of *Oppression in Punjab*.

The first eyewitness to the Harmandir Sahib attack is Devinder Singh Duggal, the man who was in charge of the Sikh Reference Library located inside the complex. According to Duggal, the army fired at the Harmandir Sahib on June 1st itself[59], not on June 5th as the government's *White Paper* claims.[60] He recalls that the firing started from the outside at 12:30 p.m., and continued for seven hours.[61] When asked if there was firing from within, Duggal stated[62]:

> *Not a single shot was fired from inside the complex. When I asked some of the boys, as to why they did not answer the firing, they replied that they were under strict orders of the Sant [Jarnail Singh] not to fire a single shot unless and until the security forces or the Army entered the holy Golden Temple.*

On the evening news over the All India Radio[63] however, a bulletin reported that there was unprovoked firing from the inside of the complex, and that the security forces showed extreme restraint and did not fire a single shot. The fact that a minimum of eight people were killed, as well as thirty-four bullet holes in the sides of the Harmandir Sahib on that first night, serve to discredit the government's tales.[64] According to Duggal, June 2nd passed peacefully with no curfew and no firing from the outside of the complex; during this time, large numbers of Sikhs were allowed to enter the Harmandir Sahib.[65] On the special day that was to follow, June 3rd, the tens of thousands of Sikhs in the Harmandir Sahib would be commemorating the martyrdom of their fifth Guru.

The thousands of pilgrims that had been allowed to collect inside the Harmandir Sahib Complex were given no warning of the sudden curfew or the ensuing army attack.[66] Although there were no restrictions on entering the city of Amritsar or even the Harmandir Sahib, it was not possible to leave. Amritsar had been sealed.[67] These people were innocent citizens who had come to pay their respects at the gurduara on one of the most significant Sikh holidays. Some came to donate food to the soup kitchen, while others stopped by to pay their respects for what they thought would be only a few minutes. These men, women, children and elderly were completely unaware of the horror that would be unleashed upon them within the next twenty-four hours.

At about 4 a.m. on June 4th, the army attack commenced once again. "Thereafter, every second the ferocity of firing increased and it continued unabated till the evening of the 6th June," Duggal states. Through a window, Duggal recalls seeing piles of dead bodies on the parikarma[68], which included those of many women and children. His vivid account of the army's attack made it clear that they were recklessly firing at and murdering the people inside the complex as if they were attacking an alien force, not citizens of their own country.[69]

According to an All Indian Sikh Students Federation member, who would not give his name out of fear for his life, there were about one hundred freedom fighters with Bhindranwale inside the Harmandir Sahib Complex, and less than one hundred arms, mostly from World War II.[70] Completely contradictory to what the *White Paper* published[71], a girl student who was one of the few to survive the massacre, also claimed that on June 4th, "...if a thousand rounds were being fired by the army from outside, then about one or one and a half rounds were fired in reply by the armed militants from inside the Temple complex."[72]

The report published by the Government of India after the attack claimed[73]:

> *A large quantity of weapons, ammunition and explosives was recovered, including automatic and anti-tank weapons. A small factory for the manufacture of hand grenades and sten guns was also found within the precincts of the Golden Temple.*

Had there been a modern arms factory manned by hundreds of terrorists, would the resistance have collapsed within two to three days? If
there *were* such factories, then where did the evidence, the weapons
and the machinery, disappear to? The myriad of such questions posed
to the Indian government by independent researchers and human
rights organizations remain unanswered even today.

Although there had been some stray firing from within the complex in
response to the army's firing from the outside, the resistance began
only after the army violated the sanctity of the Harmandir Sahib by
charging in. By the time the army entered on June 5th, nearly all of the
resistance forces had been exhausted, with only a minimal amount of
ammunition remaining.[74]

The survivors remember that at 1 a.m. on June 6th, one armored carrier
and eight tanks entered the Harmandir Sahib Complex, destroying not
only the entrances through which they came, but also the sacred marble ground on which they drove. From the tanks it was announced,
"Please come out, God's blessings are with you. We will reach you
home absolutely safe and sound." Those who were thirsty and tired
came out into the open, hoping to be returned safely to their families.
Instead, they were shot down at sight.[75]

Ram Narayan Kumar and Georg Sieberer explain in
The Sikh Struggle[76]:

> *The army which had suffered a heavy toll in three days*
> *of battle went berserk and killed every Sikh to be found*
> *inside the temple complex. They were hauled out of the*
> *rooms, brought to the corridors in the circumference of*
> *the Temple, and with hands tied to their back were shot*
> *in cold blood. Among the victims were many old men,*
> *women and children.*

As reported by Brahma Challaney of the Associated Press of America,
a large number of innocent Sikhs were killed in a barbaric manner –

their own precious turbans binding their hands behind their backs, while army officers callously shot them at point blank range.[77] The Government of India emphatically denies all of these facts, but they are corroborated by the post-mortem reports. The story of the Indian army's attack of the Harmandir Sahib shows stark similarity to accounts of Alexander the Greats' murderous empire hunting excursions. Philosophers have written that when Alexander did not spare the innocent inhabitants of a city after a victory, Aristotle wrote him a letter asking that if before a victory one is excused for killing his enemies, what excuse is there to kill innocents after the victory has been attained?[78] If the government did indeed only want to weed out the terrorists, then what is their excuse for lining up innocent men, women and children and killing them after the operation was over and the entire complex was in the army's control?

The sheer proportion of the attack leaves us in shock. As Dr. Cynthia Keppley Mahmood points out[79]:

> *The key problem was that the scale of the assault was disproportionate to the actual threat that the band of militants posed to the Indian state. There were about two hundred armed insurgents at the Complex on that day, but the army responded with some 70,000 troops who used, among other things, tanks and CS gas in the attack on the Complex.*

The story of Devinder Singh Duggal matches those of the other survivors to the exact date and approximate time. Since these people had no contact with each other, it would be nearly impossible for them to coordinate their stories prior to their interview with the members from the Citizens for Democracy team. Can it be of mere coincidence that Duggal's version of the attack parallels those of a girl student, Prithipal Singh, Joginder Singh, Giani Puran Singh, Bhan Singh, Surinder Singh, Baldev Kaur, Harcharan Singh, an A.I.S.S.F. member and several other Sikh survivors?[80]

Even if the stories of these survivors are ignored, we cannot dismiss the integrity of several human rights organizations, such as Amnesty International, Human Rights Watch Asia, and the United Nations, who have made severe accusations against the Government of India. The mere fact that thirty-seven other Sikh gurduaras around India were attacked at the same date and time[81] serves to disprove the government's statement that Operation Bluestar was executed in order to flush out Jarnail Singh and his terrorists from the Harmandir Sahib. The unimpressive series of lies proposed by the Indian government have no place amongst the poignant stories of the people who themselves witnessed the invasion and survived it. Ms. Joyce Pettigrew explains the essence of the army invasion of the Harmandir Sahib eloquently when she states[82]:

The army went into Darbar Sahib not to eliminate a political figure or a political movement but to suppress the culture of a people, to attack their heart, to strike a blow at their spirit and self-confidence.

CHAPTER 5
The True Colors of Bluestar

Truth, it is well known, is the biggest casualty in war, and few may be aware, or though aware, would not like to admit that a war is on—an undeclared, unilateral ruthless war—against hundreds of innocent defenseless men and women in far away tiny villages of Punjab from where their voices do not reach the rest of India.

Citizens for Democracy[83]

While the government claims that 675 terrorists and civilians were either killed or injured during Operation Bluestar and attacks on other Sikh gurduaras[84], conservative estimates by reputable sources and survivors range to 10,000 citizens.[85] Joyce Pettigrew reports that a senior police officer, who resigned his post as a protest against the government's actions, placed the number killed at 20,000.[86] Yet these figures are clearly very conservative when we logically approximate the number of people present. During many gurpurabs[87], the Harmandir Sahib Complex is crowded with people. Attendance at such events easily exceeds a hundred thousand devotees. The anniversary of Guru Arjan Dev Ji's martyrdom is among the most well attended gurpurabs. Any person who has attended this gurpurab will be able to confirm that during this time, there is hardly any room to move as there are so many people inside the gurduara. How can there be only 675 deaths or injuries, when the complex was completely sealed *after* letting the devotees in, while there were only a few thousand survivors (almost all of whom ended up in prison).

In conjunction with the brutal nature of the attack, the grave human rights violations that took place led the Indian government to ban even neutral agencies such as the Red Cross from entering the Harmandir Sahib Complex[88]. Press censorship had been imposed in Amritsar, with the foreign reporters and Indian journalists alike being barred from entering.[89] As there was no reliable independent source of news about the happenings in Punjab, the citizens of India as well as the people of the outside world could only know about the situation through the government-sponsored investigative report, the *White Paper*. Any independent person who sought the truth was charged with sedition, labeled as an anti-national terrorist sympathizer, and was thrown into jail.

In addition to the restrictions placed on Amnesty International, Human-Rights Watch-Asia, the British Parliamentary Human Rights Group, and even United Nations Human Rights Reporters, independent research teams from within India, comprised of Indian citizens, have been banned from investigating crimes in India. In a lecture at Cornell University in 2003, the then Attorney General of India, the Honorable Soli Sorabjee, stated that organizations such as Amnesty International and Human-Rights Watch Asia are *still* restricted from entering areas in Punjab to investigate human rights violations.[90]

Under the conditions of the International Covenant on Civil and Political Rights, to which India is party[91], United Nations representatives are permitted access into all countries to investigate claims of heinous crimes.[92] Additionally, according to the United Nations Charter of Human Rights, the Red Cross is permitted to aid the wounded inside a battle zone, even if it is in an enemy territory. What is so unbelievable is that this was not even enemy territory – it was on Indian soil that such brutalities took place. If the army truly only wanted to weed out the terrorists, why did they not allow the Red Cross to aid the thousands of innocents ?

One wonders that if the government's actions were honest, and that their own newspapers were in fact reporting nothing but the truth, then why were independent, unbiased observers not allowed to witness the conflict with their own eyes? Such action would surely serve to maintain the integrity of the Congress government and wash away any trace of doubt left in the minds of leaders across the world. Yet the inappropriate restrictions lead us to believe that the Indian government clearly had something to hide from the eyes of the international community.

Since there is a complete lack of independent, unbiased reporting on what happened in the city of Amritsar in June of 1984, we must derive the truth by comparing the government's investigative report, the *White Paper*, to the eyewitness accounts of survivors. The story begins with the unfolding of the attack on the Harmandir Sahib.

One of the greatest disputes in regards to the attack and counter attack rests in the number of arms present inside the gurduara. The *White Paper* repeatedly refers to the apparent large quantity of weapons inside the Harmandir Sahib, stating that the so-called terrorists put up a great fight. In addition to rifles, stenguns, explosives, grenades, and mines, the government claims that the Sikhs had automatic and anti-tank weapons.[94]

This was their justification for razing the Harmandir Sahib – the Sikhs of Punjab were apparently too big of a threat to the unity of the country with all of their arms and ammunition. Yet no eyewitness or frequenter of the Harmandir Sahib can remember any grenade or stengun factory, as the *White Paper* claims that there were. Rather, they insist that there were a limited number of men, and so few arms that they had to be used sparingly.[95] Further, reputable human rights workers and well-known newspapers such as *The Economist* in London have published reports stating, "Even the tally of captured weapons – fewer than 1,500 guns of all kinds in the entire state of Punjab – does little to bolster the government's allegations of a massive anti-national conspiracy against the Indian union."[96] Not only is the quantity of weapons in question, but the apparent danger of these weapons is on trial as well.

Dr. Iqbal Singh of the University of Chicago states[97]:

> *It is hard to conceive that 1500 weapons, some of pre-First World War vintage, could even remotely be a challenge to [the] world's fourth largest armed forces composed of a million soldiers, thousands of tanks, aircraft and modern artillery.*

A pamphlet published by the Committee on Human Rights, *The Turning Point: India's Future Direction?*, stated in 1985[98]:

> *With the passage of time the imposing picture of the arms buildup within the Temple has now begun to shrink in size. The heaviest arms which are claimed to have been recovered are light machine guns. Poised against the heavy tanks and armoured vehicles and the heavy guns of the Indian army, they would appear as toys. But one cannot be sure about the authenticity of even that. After all, it is no problem for the government and the army to find an assortment of arms to make an exhibit when care had been taken to keep everyone out who could report on arms being brought by the army and para-military forces from outside to make out a case after their action.*

Assuming for a moment that the *White Paper's* claims of many modern arms inside the gurduara was true, another important question arises, one that was posed by the President of India at the time as well. With the heavy surveillance and searching of every person, vehicle, and delivery truck that had been entering the vicinity of the Harmandir Sahib for over a year, how was it even possible for the supposed terrorists to sneak such a large quantity of weapons inside? Ajoy Bose reported of the civil liberties violations in his article "The Legacy of Fear," in *The Manchester Guardian*. He tells of the armed soldiers that searched even tractors and bullock carts along the highways and streets.[99] And yet the government sees no flaw in such logic. They vehemently claim that they were keeping a close watch on the suspected persons, and that at the same time, the alleged terrorists managed to sneak in a large quantity of weapons.

The President of India at the time, Zail Singh, recalls in his memoirs[100]:

> *In anguish, I asked Mrs. Gandhi what were our intelligence agencies doing all those months, when arms build-up was going on in this religious place...It was ironical, I supposed, that innocent people had to pay with their lives for the dereliction of duty by the security forces and the intelligence organs of the Government. Mrs. Gandhi had obviously no plausible answer.*

When no answer could be given as to how the alleged terrorists had even acquired such arms and ammunition, the government put forth theories stating that the terrorists had snatched them from police officers or had raided arms holdings. The most interesting theory that they proposed was that the supposed terrorists had acquired arms from some foreign country.[101] As entertaining as these theories may be, none of them are probable.

Another topic of debate in regards to the attack on Harmandir Sahib, is the hiding and protection of terrorists from the police. According to the government's *White Paper*, there were many terrorists hiding in the Harmandir Sahib under the pretext of being religious devotees.[102] The government states that all attempts to convince the Shiromani Gurduara Prabandhak Committee[103] to turn over the *wanted* men had failed.[104] Interesting it is, that few people seem to acknowledge the fact that the government ever asked any men to be turned in to the police. Dr. Subramanian Swamy, a well known member of the Indian Parliament, wrote that the Indian government kept claiming that there were terrorists inside the gurduara, but that they had only appealed to the SGPC to turn over forty men, and even then, these requests had been made over a year and a half before the events in June. Out of these men, he reported that eighteen could not even be inside the complex (they were in jail in Pakistan, in Canada or Germany, or already dead). The other twenty-two men, according to Swamy, could not be located inside of the complex by the SGPC's screening committee. He tells of how P.C. Sethi, a member of the Lower House of the Parliament later admitted these facts. Swamy states, "Since then, no further lists have been sent to the SGPC, and yet the government keeps declaring that criminals are hiding in the Temple complex."[105] Even the charges against Baba Jarnail Singh Bhindranwale were only political – he had been accused of giving inflammatory speeches.[106] In fact, the warrants for the arrest of Bhindranwale had not been made until *after* Operation Bluestar.[107] In order to take extreme measure, as the government did by storming the Harmandir Sahib, it is imperative to first charge a man with a crime, attempt to arrest him, and if *then* he does not cooperate, state that he is a criminal. Surely it must not be a crime to make speeches about injustices and human rights violations in India, a country that claims so proudly to be the world's largest democracy. The Committee on Human Rights stated[108]:

> *The most disturbing thing about the entire operation was that a whole mass of men, women and children were ordered to be killed merely on the suspicion that some terrorists were operating from the Golden Temple and other Gurdwaras. There had been no judicial verdict of guilt against definite individuals who had been taking shelter in the Golden Temple...Thus such a major military attack resulting in the massacre of largely innocent people was undertaken on mere suspicion which had been created by the statements of police and the government themselves.*

The *White Paper* reports that commanders were instructed to use the public address system for several hours at every place where alleged terrorists were suspected of hiding out, so that the army would be able to avoid the otherwise unpreventable bloodshed and destruction of the Harmandir Sahib, actions that they were supposedly very reluctant to take.[109] Yet the President of India during the attack, stated in his memoirs[110]:

> *I asked the Government whether they had issued a warning on the loudspeakers to the people inside the complex to come out, to which they replied in the affirmative. Later, I came to know that no such warning had been issued by the authorities and the Operation had been suddenly launched.*

If the government is willing to lie even to the sitting President of the country to cover their machinations and misdeeds, then how can we, the bystanders, be expected to believe what they say.

Keeping with their tradition of deception, the *White Paper* makes several claims in regards to those that were killed during the ferocious attack. The deaths of most of those who perished in the army firing were blamed on the alleged terrorists themselves. They claim that as people were preparing to surrender, the so-called terrorists shot them down.[111] Not only are these claims completely contradictory to the stories of the eye witnesses, but they lack any logic. Why would the Sikhs that were defending the Harmandir Sahib waste the little ammunition that they had on those that were surrendering? According to the survivors of the attack, the people who responded to the army's demand to reveal themselves were shot in cold blood, but by the Indian Army soldiers, not the Sikhs.[112] The only wrong-doing of these innocent Sikhs was to believe that their government would protect their right to life, liberty, and the security of person as guaranteed in the preamble of the United Nations Universal Declaration of Human Rights and the Indian Constitution.[113] How can we be expected to believe anything that the *White Paper* claims when they have made such clearly refutable statements time and time again?

Further, the *White Paper* claims that the troops exercised extreme restraint and avoided firing at the Harmandir Sahib, because this Operation was supposedly conducted to weed out terrorists, and not to attack the spirit of the Sikh people.[114] The report further states, "From the commencement of the planning stage of this operation...strict instructions had been issued to preserve the buildings."[115]

Complementing the image of destruction presented by the survivors of the government terrorism as well as the myriad of pictures of the razed buildings taken after the attack, the President of India explains the extent of the damage[116]:

> *The goldsheet covering the walls [of the Golden Temple] got pock-marked and those portions had just been replaced, as repairs to them were not possible...Even pieces of gold-sheet covering the dome had fallen off...I sent a letter to Mrs. Indira Gandhi telling her about the great dimensions of the damage that had occurred to the Akal Takht and the Golden Temple.*

A considerable amount of damage must have been done to the Harmandir Sahib in order for the gold plating to have fallen off. Dr. Devinder Singh Duggal states that the Harmandir Sahib bore at least three hundred thousand bullet marks.[117] This is the "utmost reverence" that the government claims it held while occupying the religious sanctuary.[118]

The *White Paper* also claims that the alleged terrorists themselves were responsible for setting fire to the Sikh Reference Library, which contained hundreds of irreplaceable original manuscripts and scriptures, on June 5th. It also states that the army's fire rescue was only unable to help put out the fire due to the machine-gun attacks of the supposed terrorists.[119] Yet the man who was in charge of the library, Devinder Singh Duggal, remembers it being intact when he last saw it as he was removed from the complex on June 6th. He recalls[120]:

> *On 14th June 1984 I was arrested by the army and taken inside the Golden Temple, where I was shocked to see that the Sikh Reference Library had been burnt. The*

*entire Golden Temple Complex presented a very, very
painful look. It bore at least 3 lakhs[121] of bullet marks.
The Akal Takhat was in shambles. Guru Nanak Nivas,
Teja Singh Samundri Hall, Guru Ram Das Serai and the
langar buildings had been burnt. When I left the complex on the 6th all those building were in good shape in
spite of the Army Attack.*

If most of the buildings, including the Sikh Reference Library, were
intact when the Operation ended, then how is it that they had been
reduced to ashes when Duggal was taken back? The most logical con-
clusion that can be drawn from these facts is that the army deliberately destroyed the sacred buildings *after* they had been evacuated.
Operation Bluestar was not at all an attack on a group of terrorists as
the government is so quick to claim. Rather it was an attack on the
very heart and soul of the people who fought government oppression
at the cost of their own lives.

The government then had the audacity to claim that "no women or
children were killed in the action by the troops."[122] With the tens of
thousands of innocent pilgrims killed – with the hundreds upon hundreds of reports of army brutality, in which eye-witnesses testify to the
cold blooded murder of young children and elderly women by the
troops themselves – how they were stripped naked and shot at point-
blank range – where the army has photographed women and children
with their hands tied behind their backs[123] – with the testimonies of
well respected human rights activists such as Ram Narayan Kumar and
Georg Sieberer[124] – the government has the *audacity* to tell us that no
women or children were killed by the action of the troops.

The story of infant-terrorists, as they are often referred to by the government, stands testimony to the utter falsity of such statements. It was
reported by several prominent reporters such as Gobind Thukral, that
in addition to the tens of thousands of men and women that perished
in Operation Bluestar, there were other victims – children – between
the ages of two and twelve. The story of four-year-old Rinku is a heart

wrenching one, which only *begins* with the disappearance of his mother and murder of his father by the army. Orphaned, jailed, and tortured by the government, when asked why his stomach was so big, the four-year-old replied, "Because I eat clay." Of the 39 children captured, three had been classified as "dangerous terrorists"[125]. This is the sad state of India, where children, as young as two years old, understand and experience the same fear as their parents – the fear of being kidnapped, experiencing gruesome torture, and ultimately being murdered. No doubt remains – this is certainly the most grim hour in Indian history.

We can also see that the *White Paper's* claim that the army paid great respect to the sacred gurduara while capturing the alleged terrorists is erroneous, through the numerous pictures that were taken after the attack by the army members themselves. In a Sikh gurduara, it is mandatory to cover one's head and remove one's shoes to show respect and reverence. In addition, it is most sacrilegious to drink alcohol or use tobacco in a gurduara, considering that these two acts are against the fundamental principles of Sikhism. To gain popular support for the army's actions, it was necessary for the government to portray to the public that it had done everything possible to maintain the sanctity of the Harmandir Sahib. The *White Paper* most emphatically states that the army took care to show utmost reverence and ensure that no desecration or damage was done.[126] Yet in several of the pictures taken by the army personnel themselves, we can see that the officer's heads are not covered, and that the men are wearing boots.[127] Many believe that both alcohol and cigarettes had been served by the army inside the Harmandir Sahib after the invasion. Yet most of the reporters and newspapers of the time neglected to mention this desecration. It was only later that independent reporters discovered and revealed this grave violation.

A more severe intrusion than this, the Guru Granth Sahib[128] and other religious scriptures were ripped and burnt, while urine drenched those that were not. As we discovered earlier, most of the destruction to the Harmandir Sahib happened *after* the army had secured the complex as confirmed by eyewitnesses. The army destroyed the Sikh Reference Library, and with it, religious and historical items, including original manuscripts and irreplaceable artifacts. The government's *White Paper* can truly be called "Operation Whitewash" as India's reputable national magazine, *India Today*, labeled it.[129]

As well as neglecting to record who was killed during Operation Bluestar, the Indian Army disrespected the lifeless bodies of the innocent pilgrims by dragging them by the limbs to throw them into dump trucks. With the bodies piled up and burned by the twenties (since the numbers were so high that not enough firewood was even available in the crematoriums to give a proper cremation[130]), no list of the massacred was produced to inform the families of the victims.[131]

The Citizens for Democracy report sums up the outrageousness of the attack in the following lines[132]:

> *A number of responsible men and women who were inside the Golden Temple throughout the Army action, described to us how innocent people were slaughtered like rats – first letting them enter the Complex and then declaring the curfew which prevented them from going out – thousands were thus caught unaware; finally when the survivors were asked to surrender they were shot in cold blood; our photograph would show how the hands of men were tied at their back with their own turbans, some of whom were shot. The post mortem reports show how the bullets had pierced their bodies. The eye witnesses witnessed the use of gas by the Army, the pile of dead bodies on the 'parikarma', the arrival of tanks which some of them thought were the ambulance, the hovering of helicopters at night, throwing their search-light on targets which were bombed, the wanton destruction of the Akal Takhat, the Research*

*Library and the Museum...The facts have been exposed
that the Army's 'restraint' we heard so much of and
have proved conclusively that the White Paper is after
all not so white. We learnt for the first time with amaze-
ment that the Red Cross was not allowed even to enter
the Complex to attend to the wounded, many not
allowed any water to drink died of thirst; on June 7th,
28 people were pushed inside a strong room without
any ventilation and locked up, and when the room was
opened, 14 of them were dead. Bodies were left to rot,
inside the room and then burnt. This was free India's
Jallianwala Bagh – leaving the old Jallianwala Bagh of
the British days far behind in the number killed and in
the manner of killing.*

Perhaps, if there were in fact terrorists, there was another method to
remove them from the Harmandir Sahib, a method that would prevent
the loss of so many innocent lives. President Zail Singh tells in his memoirs of how he wondered the same. He recalls asking Mrs. Gandhi if it
was not possible to give a prior warning of the attack so that the innocents may have been allowed to leave; why a curfew could not have
been imposed to stop the movement of people into the complex; why
religious leaders could not have been asked to make an appeal to the
Sikhs to protect the sanctity of the Harmandir Sahib; as to why the
Operation had been carried out on a day when it was obvious that the
maximum number of Sikhs would have collected. He states, "I told her
that if notice had been given to those pilgrims over Radio, Television,
and loudspeakers, a majority of them would have come out, including
some extremists, to surrender."[133]

If one has any intent or desire to save innocent lives, then such measures can certainly be employed. Why such warnings were not issued
hints at the carelessness towards the life of innocents that veiled
Operation Bluestar. Surely the army could have deprived those that
remained inside of food until they surrendered. If he was in fact such

a threat to the unity of the nation, it was of course also possible to shoot Baba Jarnail Singh down during one of the speeches made from atop the Langar Hall Building. Such thoughtful planning would most definitely have reduced the unprecedented loss of life. Retired Chief Justice S.M. Sikri of the Supreme court of India declared the Operation as a, "massive, deliberate and planned onslaught on the life, property and honor of a comparatively small, but easily identifiable, minority community."[134] The elaborately planned disregard for human life in Operation Bluestar cannot be overlooked, for failure to acknowledge this offense foreshadows its repetition. Though it is an imposing task to sort through all of the accounts of what occurred in Operation Bluestar, just like the gardener who wants the garden to grow, we must be willing to put forth this effort. Only then can the seeds of truth, justice and freedom from oppression grow.

CHAPTER 6
The Nameless Operation

*...the attacks on members of the Sikh Community...
far from being a spontaneous expression of "madness"
and of popular "grief and anger" at Mrs. Gandhi's
assassination as made out to be by the authorities,
were the outcome of a well-organised plan marked by
acts of both deliberate commissions and omissions by
important politicians of the Congress (I) at the top and
by authorities in the administration.*

People's Union for Democratic Rights
and People's Union for Civil Liberties[135]

Even the gruesome nature of the attack on the tens of thousands of
innocent pilgrims inside the Harmandir Sahib does not compare to
the disturbing nature of the anti-Sikh pogroms that took place after
the death of Prime Minister Indira Gandhi. On October 31st, 1984,
following the assassination of Indira Gandhi by her Sikh bodyguards,
all hell broke loose for the Sikhs. For three days straight, crazed
mobs organized by the leaders of the ruling Congress Party themselves went berserk, pulling Sikhs out of their houses, beating them
ruthlessly, throwing tires around their necks, dousing them in
kerosene, and burning them alive, a practice so familiar in the
pogroms, that the President of India referred to it as the "garland
treatment."[136] Innocent Sikh men were scalped[137], and women and
children were not spared. Next, they looted the residences and

burned whatever they did not want, including the homes of the innocent Sikhs. Further, Sikh gurduaras were vandalized all over India, with mobs desecrating their sanctity or burning them down. Any lingering integrity within the police force was diminished as they incited the angry mobs or stood idle, watching the crimes. A senior police officer stated before the Misra Commission, "The riots were engineered to teach the Sikhs a lesson."[138] Despite appeals made to the Prime Minister Designate, Rajiv Gandhi, and to the Home Minister, Narasimha Rao, the army was not called in to protect the innocent people until several days later, when the damage had already been done and the lives had already been lost.[139] When the well-known civil disobedience leader, Mohandas Gandhi, was assassinated by a Maharashtrian Hindu, prior to the formal announcement of his death the government deployed police and powerful authorities to secure the safety of all citizens. Yet this precaution was not taken in November of 1984 for the Sikhs. The death of Indira Gandhi was broadcast over the radio and printed in the newspapers without making any arrangements for the safety of the innocent Sikhs whose lives were clearly to be endangered by this news.

Subsequent to the Indian Army's attack on the Harmandir Sahib, the government of Punjab used the Special Powers Act to prohibit the publication and transmission of material that may have aroused communal zeal and impacted the maintenance of public order.[140] Essentially, the purpose of putting such restrictions in place was to protect the Hindu population, or more specifically, the government agents, from any possible backlash from the Sikh community. It is interesting that they prohibited the broadcasting and publication of material regarding the invasion of the Harmandir Sahib to protect the Hindus from a community whose representation was within 2% of the population, but did not take such action to prevent the backlash of the Hindu community against the Sikhs before announcing the assassination of Mrs. Indira Gandhi. *The Washington Post* reported the former Prime Minister, Charan Singh, of having criticized Rajiv Gandhi's reaction to the violence, declaring his "ineptness" in handling the carnage.[141]

Rather than ensuring the safety of Sikhs by protecting them against the anger of the Hindu community that was inevitably to follow, the government circulated a series of unjustified and unsubstantiated rumors following the announcement of Indira Gandhi's death on October 31st [142]:

1) The first being that the Sikhs were distributing sweets and dancing to celebrate Mrs. Gandhi's death. As independent researchers and organized committees such as the People's Union for Democratic Rights and the People's Union for Civil Liberties have found, the people spreading these rumors have admitted that they themselves did not witness Sikhs committing any such acts. These teams have found that the incidences of happiness expressed at Mrs. Gandhi's death were isolated cases, and that those that were exhibiting this behavior were people of all religious backgrounds, both Sikhs and non-Sikhs. The book *Who Are the Guilty?* insightfully states, "...these stray incidents were marginal and do not explain the wide scale explosion of indiscriminate violence against all Sikhs throughout India on the same date and the same time, which could be the result of only a well designed strategy."[143]

2) The other rumors that were circulated in order to rouse mobs against the Sikhs were that the drinking water all throughout Delhi had been poisoned, that trains full of dead Hindus had arrived at the Old Delhi Station from Punjab, and that the Sikhs were responsible for the poisoning and the alleged murders. Research teams found that police officers were traveling to various communities to spread the news of the poisoned water and the trains. It is surprising that the Delhi Police could organize and disseminate men to spread this unconfirmed news, while they found it too difficult to provide protection to the Sikhs who were being lynched and burned alive at the hands of organized mobs. Following their tradition of manipulating and lying, we find that police records of trains full of dead Hindus do not even exist. The news of this event that had been spread across all of India was later found to have been absolutely false. Although the rumors of the poisoned water and the trains were officially repudiated later, the damage had already

been done: these lies helped engender the public opinion that endorsed the violent slaughter of the Sikhs that followed within the next few days.

During the five deadly days in November, the police force showed a complete absence from the murder scenes, stood as passive spectators to the violence, or were active participants themselves in the attack on innocent Sikhs and the plundering of their shops and homes.[144] In many cases, the police arrived in towns and announced that they were not responsible for the safety of the Sikhs, who they assured, could protect themselves.[145] What is the responsibility of the police if it is not to protect the law-abiding citizens of the country? If it is to encourage mobs and provide them the means to unleash terror and execute heavy religious cleansing on innocent men, women and children, then the police did an outstanding job of fulfilling their duties and responsibilities.

S.M. Sikri, retired Chief Justice of the Indian Supreme Court provided significant evidence indicating that the police not only failed in protecting the citizens, but instigated the arson and violence themselves.[146] The People's Union for Democratic Rights and the People's Union for Civil Liberties reported that Congress leaders themselves "led and directed the arsonists and that local cadres of the Congress (I) identified Sikh houses and shops" providing them the means to kill Sikhs. Government owned vehicles, such as buses from the Delhi Transport Corporation, were used to move the miscreants from place to place on their murderous journey. They selectively set fire to houses, shops and gurduaras that were owned by Sikhs. A senior police officer brought up an excellent point[147]:

The shop signs are either in Hindi or English. How do you expect the illiterate arsonists to know whether these shops belong to Hindus or Sikhs, unless they were identified to them by someone, who is either educated or a local person?

President Zail Singh tells of how the Sikhs that had licensed arms were also left defenseless, as the police took away their weapons and then directed the mobs to attack them.[148]

The police do not accept responsibility for what happened, and yet, cannot plausibly deny being responsible. Confidential voting lists had been handed out to assailants, who used the records to identify the houses, shops, gurduaras and schools belonging to Sikhs, as the President recalled in his memoirs, and as reported in *Who Are The Guilty*[149]. These buildings were then tagged with paint-marks the night before Congress leaders would bring the mobs into the village. Had the police and government's machinery not been responsible for the acts of violence that took place, how did these criminals acquire the lists and identify the houses with paint accordingly?

The President wrote[150]:

> *One Congress leader vehemently told me of the macabre drama deliberately staged to kill members of the Sikh community as a deterrent, as also to put them in their place. Those Hindus and others, who were noticed by the police trying to protect the Sikhs, were chided, belaboured and even threatened...A Sikh was a Sikh and, if he could be cornered by death-hounds, he must be bludgeoned to death with iron rods or burnt alive. A Hindu lady telephoned my secretary to say that she had witnessed Sikhs being given the 'garland treatment,' i.e., being done to death by placing blazing motor tyres around their necks.*

It was the consistency of the crimes that made even the most ardent Congress supporter suspicious of the government's involvement. President Zail Singh further wrote[151]:

It was a strange coincidence that the iron rods used to bludgeon the victims throughout were of the same size and shape. In some States, where the influence of the north Indian Congress ruling class was not pronounced, there were little disturbances. Some states remained totally free of this taint.

Those responsible for the lives of the Sikhs that were murdered and burnt alive, knowingly and purposefully neglected their duty to protect these innocent citizens. As Justice V.M. Tarkunde explains in his *Tarkunde Report*, "there is much evidence to prove that the local Congress (I) leaders held meetings on the night of October 31st, paying 1,000 rupees to each killer, as boasted by the killers themselves."[152] Thus, in addition to the police, the real perpetrators of these crimes were the government officials themselves. In regards to the part played by the higher authorities, the People's Union for Democratic Rights and the People's Union for Civil Liberties states in their book *Who Are the Guilty?*[153]:

Men at the top in the administration and the ruling party displayed repeatedly a curious lack of concern often bordering on deliberate negligence of duty and responsibility throughout the period of October 31st to November 4th...

The authorities at the top, including the four Ministers and senior officials of the Delhi Administration were repeatedly informed about the exact situation in the city and its outskirts from the evening of October 31st. Prominent citizens, VIPs and members of the Opposition parties and people from affected localities both phoned and personally went and informed these authorities. Yet during seven valuable hours, between the time of the assassination and the time of the news of the death was made public, no security measures were taken.

N.S. Saxena, a retired police officer, wrote that had Doordarshan[154] shown footage of the violence and brutalities that had taken place on the first day of rioting, many of the rioters would have been deterred and rioting in upcoming days would have taken shape on a much smaller scale. Yet this footage was not shown until after the riots were over, and the mobs continued the murders with full force.[155] President Zail Singh remembers the television station relaying footage of highly provocative slogans such as *Khoon ka badla khoon* (blood for blood) by members of the mourning crowd at the place where Indira Gandhi's body was lying in State.[156]

Although the Congress and the Home Minister Narasimha Rao feigned an infinite number of problems when trying to mobilize the army to ensure the safety of the Sikhs, they found no trouble in lining up 4,000 men from the Indian Army, Navy and Air Force for Indira Gandhi's funeral a few days later.[157] When the army had finally been deployed and the curfew had been imposed several days later, there was no one to carry out and implement these orders, leaving the situation as terrifying as it had been before.

Army sources have confirmed that the deployment of troops followed a curious pattern. The civil authorities sent them in stages (a practice that had never been done before), almost always to an area that had already been razed by assailants.[158] A few members of the army even complained that they were not only lacking cooperation from the army and police headquarters, but that they were being deliberately misled by the police.[159] Without knowledge of where the tension and murders existed, combined with the purposeful hindering of action by the government officials, the army was essentially ineffectual.

Yet there *were* police officers and Hindus that had acted to secure the safety of their Sikh brothers. In the case of the police however, the officers' efforts were hampered from higher-ranking officials who refused to assist them in their efforts to prevent the attacks. The Hindus that helped the Sikhs escape the mobs often risked their own lives to do so. The majority of the Sikhs that have survived the attacks and killings were saved by their Hindu neighbors, who saw it as their responsibility to protect them. Credit must be given where it is due, and here, it surely is. Hundreds of Sikhs owe their lives to their compassionate and trustworthy Hindu friends. As stated before, the communal tension that was forced upon the two communities did not entirely sever ties between them. Throughout the years, many Hindus have worked, and have often risked their own lives, to protect Sikhs when they were in danger. I note again, that the problem existed between the Sikhs and the Hindu-dominated government, not between the Sikhs and the Hindus.

To justify the slaughter of thousands of Sikhs within five days, the new Prime Minister, Rajiv Gandhi, Mrs. Gandhi's son, proclaimed, "there are always tremors when a great tree falls."[160] Yet when a Maharashtrian Hindu assassin killed Mohandas Gandhi, the earth did not tremble for the Maharashtrian Hindus. Was this civil disobedience leader a smaller tree than Indira Gandhi?[161] The reality of the situation, as eloquently stated by a later Prime Minister of India, Mr. Atal Bihari Vajpayee, was simply, "…that it is when the earth shakes that trees fall."[162]

In addition to the tens of thousands of lives that were lost at the Harmandir Sahib, the organized attacks claimed at least 2,733 Sikhs in Delhi alone. Yet this is only the official version of how many were murdered, in only one of the hundreds of cities in India. Mary Anne Weaver replayed Rahul Bedi's example of how the police intentionally distorted the number of people killed, in the Christian Science Monitor on November 15th, 1984. She reported[163]:

> *Mr. Bedi says he arrived at Trilokpuri early Friday afternoon to find the entrance sealed by police constables who said, "Nothing much was happening. It's all over. Maybe one or two people had been killed." Bedi and the other reporter made their way to Block 32 and found the road leading to the temple 'carpeted with bodies, two or three deep, for a distance of nearly 50 feet.'*

Inderjit Singh Jaijee reports in his book, *Politics of Genocide*[164]:

> *Delhi is a large sprawling city and if one adds the number of Sikhs killed in scattered localities and in transit, the number would be a minimum of 8,000 and might cross 10,000...The cumulative figure of those killed during the November, 1984 genocide all over India would be around 20,000.*

As Amitav Ghosh, a Hindu novelist and a distinguished Professor at Queens College in New York, wrote in *The New Yorker* magazine, "entire neighborhoods were gutted."[165]

With the Indian government disposing of or cremating most of the bodies without reporting the deaths, the actual number of Sikhs that were murdered by the government will never be known.

The curious neglect of responsibility and concern by the government on several different levels resulted in the massive loss of Sikh lives. The religious cleansing that ensued throughout the country in places where the Congress was in control is absolutely inexcusable, especially in a country that proclaims itself a democracy. Effectively, between October 31st and November 3rd, a government did not exist within India, as every force seemed paralyzed in the effort to save lives. Men were beaten and covered in kerosene to be burnt alive by mobs that were assisted, both covertly and overtly, by the government. Children were killed, and women were raped. At least 50,000 people were displaced with tens of thousands of Sikh homes, gurduaras and businesses being burnt to the ground. The Sikhs in the Delhi police (20%) were locked up in order to suppress any attempt to control the organized attacks.[166] Like the deployment of the army, the setting up of refugee camps was greatly delayed, and when they *were* created, they were closed within a week. Until this day, the judicial system refuses to admit the government's involvement with the crimes.

The perpetrators of the loot, arson, rape, and abduction were not prosecuted. According to the President, even those assailants that had been initially arrested had been released on ridiculously low bail or had been freed of charges on the intervention of political leaders.[167] As Amnesty International claims, "…nor have any of the accused policemen and politicians been brought to justice."[168] The officials responsible for the slaughter of thousands of Sikhs remain in the administration today, not having suffered any punishment for the murder of innocent citizens of their own country; in fact, several have been rewarded for their deeds with promotions.[169]

CHAPTER 7
Torture in India

The police took away my husband on 11.11.84
giving no reason for arrest, not saying where he was
being taken. On 13.11.84 Ludhiana Police came to tell
me that my husband was very ill and I should go with
them. Reaching there I found that he was dead, both
his arms were broken, there were many injuries on
the testicles, the legs had been stretched to such an
extent that the body had got torn and his intestines
had come out. The body had fallen apart so it could
not be brought home for cremation. There was no
FIR[170], he was not presented before any Court, he was
arrested without warrant and there was no witness
like the Sarpanch when he had been taken away.

Gurmit Kaur (age 32), widow of Karnail Singh[171]

As the international community turns a blind eye to the situation in the east, "torture remains a pervasive and daily routine in every one of India's 25 states", as Amnesty International has clearly reported.[172] It is the same institution that was created for the protection of the people that is, ironically, most heavily participating in the violation of human rights. Persuaded by the Government of India, it is the police force and the National Army that are responsible for the torture, rape and murder of minorities. The image of the government lies torn, with citizens well aware of the atrocities that have been committed against innocent people. Just as Hitler encouraged the slaughter of gypsies and homosexuals but targeted the Jews, Indira Gandhi pushed for the murder of Christians and Muslims, but targeted the Sikhs. The Citizens for Democracy report to the nation states[173]:

India is the only country which did not sign the new UN convention against torture and other cruel, inhuman or degrading treatment as punishment. The rulers who say that they believe in democracy, secularism, freedom of worship, social justice, and human rights have themselves enacted black laws and have let loose unabashed State terrorism which has been unleashed specially on the Sikhs – because they are Sikhs.

The Government of India took the official position that all Amritdhari Sikhs, those who have been baptized into the Sikh religion (and who are by that baptism required to wear a kirpan[174]), are by definition terrorists. It is worth noting that most of the Sikh legislators and ministers, members of parliament, the state Chief Ministers, and the Central Home Ministers, have been Amritdhari Sikhs, as was the President of India at the time of Operation Bluestar, Zail Singh. It may be further noted that court after court in the USA, Canada, the UK and many other countries, have upheld the right of observing Sikhs to wear a kirpan.[175] In the words of Judge J. Painter of an Ohio Court of Appeals, "To be a Sikh is to wear a kirpan – it is that simple."[176] In contrast to this, an issue of the Indian Army Bulletin (No. 153), "Baat Cheet", contains clear instructions to treat every Amritdhari Sikh as a terrorist[177]:

Any knowledge of the 'Amritdharis' who are dangerous people and pledged to commit murders, arson, and acts of terrorism should immediately be brought to the notice of the authorities. These people may appear harmless from outside but they are basically committed to terrorism. In the interest of all of us their identity and whereabouts must always be disclosed.

While amritdhari Sikhs have been officially targeted, the story is no different for un-baptized Sikhs. Like a recurring nightmare, the pattern of genocide is one that repeats itself village after village after village: arrest innocent Sikh men and take them to an interrogation center, giving their families no information on their whereabouts. At this "safe house," use inhumane methods of torture such as the ghotna[178] and belna[179], to destroy the man's body and crush his spirit. Refuse to give him food and water until he is so hungry and thirsty that he will eat his own feces and drink his own urine. If water *is* given, taunt him first – bring a glass to his mouth and then withdraw it. Allow him no more than two minutes to go to the lavatory, and if he is late, beat him mercilessly. The prisoners are to be kept in solitary confinement at all times unless they are undergoing interrogation, a common euphemism for torture. This Sikh's house is to be raided again and again, with the police taking anything of value and destroying anything that they cannot use. Question the women and children on the whereabouts of their husbands and fathers, and when they cannot answer your questions, beat and rape them. Set their fields on fire, destroying more than just their hopes of eating. Watch closely, as they physically and emotionally starve to death, with the head of the house missing, and with him, disappearing any hope of life or survival. By murdering able-bodied Sikh males, the Government of India kills the women and children that are dependent on them[180]:

Torture is our cultural heritage. Grisly tales from the ancient and feudal ages abound and today's journalism is often no more than a repetition of yesterday's history...torture is the major and at times, sole, weapon of the country's police. Torture is used to extract information, to settle old scores or to "teach a lesson" to persons. As interrogation generally takes place away from public gaze, very little restraint is exercised.

Let us not forget that women and children are subjected to the same torture. In the last week of August 1991, for example, the 200 victims

53

of extreme police brutality in the Village of Kathunangal included 10-year-old Kulbir Singh, and the deaf and dumb Mohan Singh. Women such as Gurmeet Kaur were beaten with iron rods in the stomach by Batala Police officers. She told the press that she had been beaten, subjected to extreme torture (from which she was unable to stand up), molested and threatened to be killed.[181] The women and young children tell their poignant tales with tears in their eyes, but resolve in their hearts, for they refuse to give up the fight for their rights.

They tell the grotesque tales of sadistic, inhumane torture; of how the police pull the victims' flesh with pliers, burn their skin with hot irons, boil them alive, gang rape women, pierce their feet with hot iron rods, blast away parts of their arms and legs (so much so that the bone is exposed), whip them with leather belts, gouge their eyes out, stretch them until their abdomen rips open, revealing their intestines, cut chunks of their skin away and sprinkle salt in the wounds, insert sticks covered with chilly powder into the anus, starve them for days, and bandage their eyes so tightly that they go blind. If it was not for the pictures, one might find these horrific stories quite unbelievable.

Three stories of such victims of police aggression were given during an interview of Baba Jarnail Singh Bhindranwale by Surinderjit Singh Bains in 1983[182]:

> The police took Kulwant Singh of Nagoke in their custody, hung him upside down and pierced his body with heated steel rods. They broke him joint by joint, broke his right leg and then shot him. They reported that there had been a police 'encounter.'...

> The police tied up the penises of Sukhdev Singh and Jasbir Singh, both from Isapur village. Their bodies got bloated. The police tore off their flesh with pliers, pulled flesh from their upper arms, tore out their eyes and then shot them...

All the ten nails from the hands as well as from the feet
of Gurmeet Singh of Dhulkot were extracted with pliers
and salt sprinkled over the wounds. Candles were lit
under his hands and he was burnt. Then he was shot...

Subsequent to the Second World War in which Hitler's army committed grave crimes against humanity, the Geneva Convention in 1949 set restrictions on the maltreatment of prisoners. It prohibited mutilation, cruel treatment and torture, in addition to an attack on personal dignity through humiliating and degrading treatment. Further, it rejected the passing of sentences and the carrying out of executions without prior judgment by a court. In 1975, the United Nations General Assembly adopted a declaration in which all acts of torture were prohibited.[183]

Not surprisingly, the government's reasons for bringing these Sikhs in for interrogation are precisely those for which they are forbidden to do so. Hundreds of thousands of Sikhs were tortured at the hands of the Punjab Police to punish them for their vocal objections to the tyranny and injustice in the government. Even more young boys and men were captured and tortured simply because they were Sikhs. With the presence of international laws, the Police either denied ever holding these Sikhs in their custody (which was simple since records of their entrance into the facilities did not exist[184]), or killed them before they could file reports.

The story of Amrik Singh takes place in the quiet village of Shutrana, district Patiala. Approached by Surjit Singh Sarpanch, an informer or 'cat' of the Punjab Police, this tractor mechanic refused to pay 20,000 rupees by means of extortion on May 8th, 1995. The following day, Amrik Singh and his brother, Bhagwant Singh, were approached by the police Station Head Officer, Jaspal Singh, and several other policemen at 10 a.m. while they were working. A crowd that had gathered outside of their shop witnessed the police taking the brothers away in a police vehicle. At 8 p.m. that night, the Assistant Sub-Inspector, Gurdev Singh, Surjit Singh, Jaspal Singh and several other policemen came to the station drunk:

> *Amrik Singh was stripped, kicked and struck with lathis.*[185]
> *His legs were pulled apart repeatedly until they were*
> *disjointed. Electric shocks were administered on Amrik*
> *Singh's tongue, ears and penis. All the while the police*
> *declared again and again that they were teaching*
> *Amrik Singh a lesson for defying a police "cat". Finally*
> *the police left the unconscious Amrik Singh and his*
> *brother alone in the lock-up. Bhagwant Singh believes*
> *that his brother's arms and legs were broken. On May 10,*
> *the ASI Gurdev Singh had the brothers taken to the*
> *Shutrana Police Chowki, some 7 km away. They were*
> *kept there without food or water and again that evening*
> *around 8 p.m. the ASI, the "cat", and other policemen,*
> *all drunk, dragged Amrik Singh out of the lock-up and*
> *began to kick him. Bhagwant Singh watched from*
> *his cell and pleaded with the policemen to spare his*
> *brother. Amrik Singh died under the kicks and blows of*
> *the police. The ASI removed the cord from the waist-*
> *band of Amrik Singh's underwear, tied it around Amrik*
> *Singh's neck and dragged him back to the lock-up.*

When Inder Singh, father of Amrik and Bhagwant, went to the police station on May 11th, he was told that his son had committed suicide, and that if he wanted to live, he should comply with the police version of the story. Both Bhagwant Singh and Inder Singh were then made to sign statements under the threat of death. At 5 p.m. the body was brought back to the police station, where Inder Singh was told to take it and cremate it without telling anyone, under the threat of death, once again. While Amrik Singh's body was being cremated, the police surrounded the village to make sure that no pictures of the mutilated body would be taken.[186]

Hundreds of thousands of innocent Sikh men and women have suffered in this way. Most women did not even receive the bodies of their deceased husbands and sons because the police either denied detaining them, or because the bodies were too disfigured to be identified. Government relief efforts are almost non-existent, and compensation for the death of a family member at the hands of the police is not provided, because records of detention do not exist.

The use of torture in India continues unabated until this day, with the overt approval of leading politicians and policemen. It is evident that even the justice system openly approves of the use of torture, as retired Chief Justice Ranganath Misra remarked, "third degree methods are justified."[187] If *we* also shut our eyes to the mass religious cleansing that occurs in India, then we are ourselves approving of murder. Public opposition to the legal genocide in India is quite possibly the only hope of survival for innocent minorities whose cries will otherwise be stifled by torture, rape and murder.

CHAPTER 8
Disappearances in Punjab

The disappeared have floated away as ash on Punjab's rivers or been carried skyward as smoke into Punjab's scorching heavens. The few bits of evidence we have shock and repel us: a photo of a heap of partially-burned bodies, eerily reminiscent of the Holocaust... another grainy Polaroid print of a wild dog tearing at the charcoal remains of a human leg...India is a place where innocent people die, where canals are clogged with bodies and crematoria sweep away nameless ashes, where human rights workers disappear or are thrown in jail. It is both a cradle and a grave.

Dr. Cynthia Mahmood, University of Notre Dame[188]

While the Government of India strongly denies all allegations, independent research teams as well as human rights organizations such as Amnesty International have proven without a shred of doubt that illegal abductions, extra-judicial killings as well as mass cremations have occurred in Punjab.[189] Due to the fact that the abduction of an individual is never officially recorded by the police, there is no effective system to disprove denials of involvement in disappearances. Violence, murder and lying are the tools used to first abduct innocent Sikh men and young boys, and then make them vanish.

Mary Anne Weaver from the Christian Science Monitor points out[190]:

The pattern in each village appears to be the same. The Army moves in during the early evening, cordons a village, and announces over loudspeakers that everyone must come out. All males between the ages of 15 and 35 are trussed and blindfolded, then taken away. Thousands have disappeared in the Punjab since the Army operation began. The Government has provided no lists of names; families don't know if sons and husbands are arrested, underground or dead.

In the torture chamber, the man's insignificant existence allows the officers to do with him as they wish.[191] Their unchecked and unchallenged authority leaves the man's life and the lives of those that are heavily dependent on him in the hands of brutal, merciless men. As the Khalsa Human Rights organization reported[192]:

Many cases of disappearances result in death. Disfigured bodies found in canals, by railway tracks and roadsides are testimony to the cover-up of state murder that is so much a part of everyday life in some parts of India. If suspicion of the killing is successfully laid at the feet of the police, it is often denied or invalidated by one of two improbable excuses; that whilst trying to escape he was shot or that he died in an encounter. An encounter, according to the security forces, is where a person is killed during a clash between security personnel and armed militant groups. Members of the security forces are allegedly ambushed and during the crossfire the suspect is killed. It is worth nothing that, according to Amnesty International (based on newspaper reports), in 1990 alone, encounters claimed the lives of 346 Sikh militants but only 25 police officers. The interpretation of an encounter by human rights groups is that a suspected militant is either arbitrarily killed or dies as a result of severe torture and the security forces cover up the murder by claiming the person died in an encounter.

Thousands of Sikhs have died at the hands of the lawless police under the false pretense that they were rebelling against the security forces. The numerous pictures taken of innocent victims that have been tortured to death, with imprints of hot irons on their bodies, their eyes gouged out or their abdomens stretched so much that the intestines spill out, serve to prove that "all is *not* well in India."[193]

Following the brutal attack on the Harmandir Sahib, the Indian government banned all human rights agencies from entering parts of Punjab. Neutral organizations made unabated efforts to investigate the violations in India, yet their recommendations fell on deaf ears. Furthermore, private investigations through organizations such as the Human Rights Wing of the Akali Dal were impeded with the intervention of the Punjab police and the High Courts. Members of these local human rights associations were threatened by the Police, and were repeatedly told to cease their investigations. When these humanitarians refused to give in to the corrupt and malicious dealings of the government, they too ended up amongst the disappeared.[194] As they could not prove that their fathers, sons or husbands were dead, the families of victims could not gain compensation for their deaths, complete transfer of property, or even get approval to have access to their bank accounts.[195]

The Human Rights Wing of the Akali Dal released a press note in January of 1995 on its findings in regards to the disappearances and illegal cremations that were becoming a part of everyday life for the Sikhs in Punjab. On the basis of firewood purchase records collected meticulously from the cremation grounds in the cities of Amritsar, Patti and Tarn Taran, the report suggested that the police had cremated 25,000 unclaimed bodies in Punjab. In addition to bringing forth these reports, the organization produced evidence that these bodies were actually those of Sikhs that had disappeared, and proved that the police had illegally cremated these people after they had been abducted and then extra-judicially executed.[196]

The Human Rights Wing argued, how could the police capture and execute a Sikh on the grounds that he was a terrorist, and then later claim that he was unidentifiable? In order to execute and cremate someone, should the police not know who they have killed and what crime this person has committed, and keep such facts on record? Further, the press release explained that the police had been cremating these bodies in violation of rule 25.38 in chapter 25 of the Punjab Police Rule 1934, under the Police Act of 1861, which clearly provides the procedure to be followed when dealing with an unidentified body.[197]

It was the arbitrary slaughtering of innocent Sikhs that led Jaswant Singh Khalra, General Secretary of the Human Rights Wing, to file a petition[198] in the Punjab and Haryana High Court for further independent investigations into both the illegal killings by the police, as well as the cremation of unidentified individuals. Yet the court dismissed the petition on the grounds that Khalra had no *locus standi*[199] in the investigations, and that the families of the disappeared should themselves file such petitions.[200]

By investigating the pattern of genocide by the Punjab Police, individuals such as Jaswant Singh Khalra, were endangering their own lives. Khalra was warned explicitly by the Senior Superintendent of Police at Tarn Taran, Ajit Singh Sandhu, that it "was easy to make one more disappear."[201] On September 6th, 1995, eight months after publishing the report on the disappeared and requesting further investigations into the cases of the missing, Jaswant Singh Khalra himself became one of the disappeared. Around 9:15 a.m., the Punjab Police abducted Khalra from outside his home in Kabir Park, Amritsar, while he was washing his car.[202] To this day he has not been produced in court despite the request of Amnesty International and the United States Congress, a demand by the Supreme Court of India, and a writ of habeas corpus by his wife, who all remain uninformed of his whereabouts. An Indian SPO (special police officer), Kuldip Singh, who was in charge of Jaswant Singh Khalra's custody, and witnessed his torture and the dumping of Khalra's body in the Harike canal, provided a formal statement against the Punjab Police to the CBI[203] on March 2nd, 1998.[204] The CBI's decision to dismiss Kuldip Singh's statement[205] provides clear evidence of the influence and control of the Punjab Police and stands testimony to the corruption in India. In a letter to President Clinton, 33 congressmen wrote of Kuldip Singh's fear of being abducted by the police, in addition to narrating the killing of Khalra.[206]

It is through fear and intimidation that the Indian government manages to keep its unlawful activities concealed so well. With human rights organizations and activists afraid of the government's reaction to their investigations, very few humanitarians will work to reveal the truth about Khalra or the illegal killings and cremations even today.

The Supreme Court ordered that the Central Bureau of Investigation should inquire into the allegations against the Punjab Police. Finding that the investigation revealed a "flagrant violation of human rights on a mass scale," the Court requested the National Human Rights Commission to "have the matter examined in accordance with law."[207] Yet the mandate and the scope of the NHRC investigation took several years to elucidate, with the police hindering any and all progress. Even when the conditions were finally clarified, the NHRC proved ineffective in taking action against the perpetrators of human rights violations for several reasons. Primarily, the organization was restricted from investigating the wrongdoings of security forces, investigating cases that were more than a year old, or making any form of policy. These limitations rendered the NHRC almost completely handicapped from doing any work that would expand human rights in India. Further, the reliability and success of investigations was greatly impeded by the fact that the members of the NHRC fact-finding team had been hand picked by the same government that they had been chosen to investigate.[208]

The Committee for Coordination on Disappearances in Punjab (CCDP) was created on November 9th, 1997, for the purpose of both investigating disappearances across the state, and for lobbying for India to change its domestic laws to conform to those of the United Nations in regards to torture, enforced disappearances, accountability, and compensation to victims.[209] In 1998, this committee founded the People's Commission, which served to investigate the complaints of illegal abductions, torture, enforced disappearances, extra-judicial executions and illegal cremations.[210]

Headed by K.J. Reddy, a retired judge of the Supreme Court of India and former Chairman of the Law Commission (and later Justice Jaspal Singh when Justice Reddy became ill), this committee included D.S. Tewatia, former Chief Justice of the Calcutta High Court and H. Suresh, a retired judge of the Bombay High Court. Comprised of three extremely reputable and respected men from the Indian Judicial system, this committee was clearly a credible organization that could competently investigate the human rights abuses.

Yet after their first meeting in the beginning of August, 1998, the Director General of the Punjab Police appealed to the High Court to ban the People's Commission before their second meeting, which was to be held in Ludhiana from the 23rd to the 25th of October. The petition stated that the commission posed a serious threat to India's national security interests, and that it intended to undermine India's judiciary system by setting up one that paralleled it. The reality is that the People's Commission was created to initiate and complete what the official Indian Judiciary system refused to do time and time again: investigate the grave human rights abuses of a country and a government against its own citizens. The Supreme Court of India intervened on this matter, and on September 10th gave the National Human Rights Commission complete control over the investigation in Punjab. The People's Commission, with no legal authority to conduct investigations, disbanded shortly thereafter.

Even until 2003, the National Human Rights Commission had not heard testimony in any of the 2,097 specific cases of illegal cremations referred to it by the Supreme Court of India in December of 1996.[211] The stated purpose of the NHRC was to provide compensation to families that could prove that their fathers or brothers had been extra-judicially executed. How could a family prove that the government had murdered their loved ones, when records of their arrest and detention did not exist? This catch-22 left women and children without homes, money or even food; not only had they lost their loved ones to the government pogroms, but they also lost any hope of survival. In 1999, Amnesty International wrote to the Chair of the Human Rights Commission, explaining that, "looking exclusively at only those cases where there is proof of illegal cremation by the police would exclude a vast number of Human Rights violations which have been reported from the state..."[212]

The components of redress as clearly stated in Article 19 of the *United Nations Declaration on the Protection of All Persons from Enforced Disappearance*, include much more than simply the compensation to the victims of human rights violations. As defined by Amnesty International, redress is inclusive of restitution, compensation, rehabilitation, and satisfaction and guarantees of non-repetition.[213] In *India: A vital opportunity to end impunity in Punjab*, Amnesty International reports[214]:

The awarding of compensation does not relieve the state of the need to admit responsibility for human rights violations and to bring perpetrators to justice. Similarly, it does not bring to an end the ordeal of the relatives of the victim who, in the absence of justice for those responsible, may continue to face harassment and further human rights violations.

The measures for providing redress are completely unthinkable in the context of the Indian government, where the legal guardians are themselves the oppressors, themselves the prosecutors, themselves the jury, and themselves the so called upholders of justice. In such a situation, forgetting about all of the above methods of redress, is it too much to ask of a supposedly democratic government to allow the families of victims to live with minimal dignity; where a Sikh woman can leave her home without the fear of being kidnapped, taken to a jail and raped?

Not only did the government-sponsored National Human Rights Commission make it almost impossible for a family to receive compensation for the death of a relative, but it also neglected the issue of future human rights violations. In addition, the mandate of the NHRC provided only for it to make inquiries in Amritsar, though it was clear from the report published by the Committee for Coordination on Disappearances in Punjab that illegal mass cremations had taken place in almost all of the major cities in Punjab, such as Faridkot, Kapurthala, Ludhiana, Mansa, Moga, and Zira.[215]

What is required of the Indian government in the current situation is very clear. The *United Nations International Covenant on Civil and Political Rights (ICCPR)*[216] states in Article 2 that it is imperative for a country to ensure the rights provided in the ICCPR, which include the guarantee to the right to life, safeguards against torture and arbitrary detention, and redress to victims of human rights violations. When addressing the issue of the right to life, the ICCPR's Human Rights Committee has specifically commented on disappearances as a violation, and the need to create "effective facilities and procedures to investigate thoroughly cases of missing and disappeared persons in circumstances which may involve a violation of the right to life." Articles 13 and 14 of the *United Nations Declaration on the Protection of All Persons from Enforced Disappearance*[217] also implicitly state that allegations of enforced disappearances should be investigated thoroughly, and that those responsible should be prosecuted in accordance with their violation.

Bound by these covenants, India is obligated to conduct impartial investigations into the crimes of the police against the people of Punjab, and provide relief to families of victims. Yet, they have done exactly the opposite[218]:

Against the backdrop of these international standards, Amnesty International has been concerned at consistent attempts by both the State Government of Punjab and the Central Government to impede investigation, prose-

cution and reparation for past human rights violations in Punjab. Many of the obstructive actions of the state and central governments as well as the police have been documented by Amnesty International in the past.

Backed by government officials the Punjab Police force continues to harass, arrest, and torture Sikhs illegally even today. As Amnesty International reported in 2002, "Security forces continued to enjoy virtual impunity for human rights abuses as a result of provisions contained in special security laws, including POTA[219]..." Not only have they escaped punishment for their heinous acts of violence and terrorism, but these government officials and police officers have been lauded for their efforts to weed out the Sikhs. Ram Narayan Kumar and Dr. Cynthia Mahmood state in their report, *Disappearances in Punjab and the Impunity of the Indian State*[220]:

Despite public proclamations as to the democratic nature of the Indian state and its commitments to protect human rights, the Indian Government's treatment not only of the Sikh population of Punjab but of human rights workers attempting to investigate abuses undermined its credibility. A human tragedy on the probable scale of many of the great tragedies of history has occurred in Punjab, and we do a severe disservice to those who have suffered and to those who yet may suffer when we ignore evidence to the effect that all is not well in India...We ask that India be urged to live up to its founding ideals by allowing and indeed supporting a full-scale accounting of atrocities in Punjab as a first step toward accountability, healing, and the restoration of democracy. We believe that respect for Human Rights and accountability for abuses thereof will be the only long-term guarantee of stability and peace in this important and volatile – and now nuclear – region of the world.

CHAPTER 9
The Lawlessness of the Police

Human Rights becomes secondary in conditions when men were more concerned about their own safety and the safety of their property. In the present situation, human rights take a back seat.

Mr. K.P.S. Gill, Chief of Punjab Police
(later Director General of Police)[221]

With virtually no opposition or superior check placed on the force, the officers of the Punjab Police assumed control over the state and the citizens of Punjab, as President's Rule was enacted. Control in this sense, literally, means control. The Punjab Police did not bring order, peace or justice to the already troubled state. Rather, they unleashed a reign of terror and fear that struck the hearts of the Sikhs that were already suffering from the undeniable lack of human rights and equality in the state. Inderjit Singh Jaijee lamented, "If only it could have been some tournament match on a chessboard. But it wasn't: the pawns were men, women and children and the most tragic victim was respect for the rule of law."[222]

Retired Justice Ajit Singh Bains, a man who by virtue of serving on the Punjab and Haryana High Court knew the ins and outs of the Indian system quite thoroughly, wrote in 1992 from Burail Jail in Chandigarh where he was himself being held,[223, 224]:

The state uses this method [terrorism] in several ways, two of which have gained much notoriety. The first is

*the direct and indiscriminate use of terror by the state
against the people in killings through "fake encounters",
the torture of individuals in police stations and interrogation centres, extortion through arrests or threats of
imprisonment or rape, and various other acts of violence against the people. The state also finances non-
governmental, specialized terrorist organizations to carry out various forms of intimidation such as bombings,
kidnappings, hijackings and indiscriminate killings. The
aim of the latter is to create an atmosphere of anarchy
and violence so that, out of frustration, the people
absolve the state for its direct use of violence and other
means of repression.*

Although constitutionally President's Rule can only be imposed for
a period of six months, the reign of terror lasted much longer. The
police had as one of their goals the longevity of President's Rule, for
this indirectly implied police rule. With a state government completely absent from the scene, the law was left in the hands of the lawless
police. Even when the elections were eventually held in 1992, the
need of the Punjab Police to prevent Akali leadership from winning
elections was evident. Here, the police managed to postpone elections for three months to ensure that the Congress would win at the
polls instead of the Akali party. During this three-month period, Akali
nominees were killed, those that were likely to vote for Akali candidates were arrested, candidates were threatened, and many were not
even allowed to turn in their nomination forms.

Unrigged and legitimate elections did not exist in Punjab. With the
Akali Party boycotting the elections in 1992 to protest the murders of
several Sikh candidates[225] and with the overall sabotaging of the elections, the Congress government came into power in Punjab with a
mere 23.8% of the electorate voting[226], and with a turnout of 5-20% in
rural constituencies.[227] Even these numbers did not represent legitimate
voting. As Dr. Farooq Abdullah, former Chief Minister of Jammu and

Kashmir, said, "The Punjab elections were fake; people did not vote. Security forces masquerading as people did."[228] With the lack of true democracy in Punjab from Indira Gandhi's reign onward, the Punjab Police held complete and unchallenged control. They openly indulged in murders, torture and extortion against anyone who they deemed an enemy of the state; most often, those that opposed their rule.

As a police officer has admitted himself, torture methods are employed on Sikhs because getting an alleged militant convicted legally is so difficult.[229] These officers continually attribute this difficulty in convicting Sikhs to the lack of people who are willing to provide evidence, rather than to the simple and logical explanation that these Sikhs are innocent.

In March of 1988, the Indian Parliament's Upper House approved and passed the 59th amendment to the Indian Constitution, which in effect enabled the central government to extend President's Rule in the state beyond one year, to impose emergency on the basis of "internal disturbance", and to suspend Article 21 of the Indian Constitution, which guarantees that no person shall be deprived of life or liberty except through procedures that are in accordance with the law.[230]

Cynthia Keppley Mahmood explains in *Writing the Bones*[231]:

> *Punjab was then declared a "Disturbed Area" under the Disturbed Areas Act of 1991. This astonishing move, though unheralded in the international press, meant that India was legally suspending protection of the right to life against arbitrary violation in one of its key states.*

The passing of similar legislation such as the Armed Forces Special Powers Act, Punjab Disturbed Areas Act, and the Terrorist Affected Areas (Special Courts) Act, to name a few, allowed for the suspension of almost all laws protecting the life and dignity of minorities in India. They allowed for search and seizure to take place without a warrant, allowed security forces to destroy an area on the mere *suspicion* that it was a terrorist hideout, and allowed for the killing of a suspected person without evidence, and with total immunity from prosecution. Contrary to the norms in a civilized society where you are presumed innocent until proven guilty, the Terrorist and Disruptive Activities Prevention Act (TADA) officially placed the onus of proving their innocence on the alleged terrorists. It denied the citizen bail and allowed the police to keep him in their custody for as long as the officers wished. To make it virtually impossible for the accused to gather evidence of their innocence, prisoners from one state were often kept in jails in distant states.

Such acts and legislation continue to plague India's Constitution, depriving citizens of the basic human rights as stated in the United Nations Declaration of Human Rights. Although TADA lapsed in 1995, the Prevention Of Terrorism Act (POTA) was passed in 2001, extending the detention of the arrested for 180 days without even filing a charge sheet, placing the burden of proof of innocence on the accused, making statements by police officers admissible as evidence, stating that the accused is guilty until proven innocent, and instituting other oppressive measures.[232]

As international human rights workers have testified, the compilation of hit lists is a common practice for the Punjab Police[233]. The pattern of aggression against those on the hit lists follows the same, terrifying pattern. A man is abducted from his home or from his work and taken into police custody, where he is secretly kept for days, weeks, or months. Murder after murder after murder is pinned on his name, and when the price on his head can go no higher, the policeman kills him in a staged encounter. This allows not only for the police to rid entire towns and villages of those who oppose their tyrannical rule (first through murdering men and attributing these killings to the captured man, and then by killing the wanted man himself), but it also allows for them to collect large sums of money (sometimes greater than the officer's annual salary itself, as official records have shown) as bounty. The theme remains unchanged throughout the years: they kill a man, and therefore he is a militant.[234]

On August 30th, 1988, the Director General of Police, Mr. K.P.S. Gill, put up a list of 53 "Wanted Dead or Alive" men and their addresses, with a bounty of between 25,000 and 100,000 rupees. It stated, "Reward for apprehension/liquidation of wanted terrorists/extremists as mentioned against the name here are hereby sanctioned..." The Director General of Police himself was encouraging the *liquidation* of men who were supposed terrorists and extremists.[235]

> For these and other such services, officers of the Punjab
> Police are given awards and honors. Estimates as to the
> number of awards given range from 1.5 million to 2.0
> million, which is considerably higher than the number
> of awards given to the combined Axis and Allied forces
> during both World Wars.[236]

The system for dodging punishment or accounting for the gross number of disappearances and murders in Punjab is quite simple. Even when a case is filed in the courts demanding the police to produce a corpse or detainee, it gets transferred from court to court, district to district, and even state to state, delaying the proceedings for years. Further, when senior police personnel and even judges fail to appear, court dates are pushed to later and later times. The exiguous evidence that existed, a gruesome photo showing the man or women's tortured body, a mother, son, daughter or widow's poignant story, the horrifying testimony of a man who witnessed the torture of the Sikh, also become tarnished or disappear with time. After the case has been prolonged for a period of five to twelve years, it is simply dismissed.

With the thousands upon thousands of illegal murders every year, the Punjab Police soon ran out of places to hide the corpses of the innocents that they had butchered. Ram Narayan Kumar and Dr. Cynthia Mahmood explain[237]:

> Punjab's irrigation canals had become the dumping
> grounds for bodies of disappeared citizens as well as
> of executed militants, and the state government of

Rajasthan to the south formally complained of dead bodies floating down from Punjab. News reports said that the dead bodies of Sikhs, many with hands and feet tied together, were being fished out when water in-flow channels were dredged for repairs. These reports stood in contradiction to the government claim that the missing Sikhs were all militants who had fled to Pakistan or abroad to continue the separatist insurgency. For a tiny minority this was a possible scenario, but the allegations of executions and disappearances were by that time numbering in the thousands. Interviewing their relatives, human rights workers found it impossible to believe that all were militants escaping into hiding overseas. Most of the relatives affirmed strongly that the victims had no connections with politics or insurgency.

In one of the irrigation canals in Punjab, the Sirhind Canal, human rights workers found nineteen bodies over a nineteen kilometer range. Given that there are over 5,000 kilometers of canals system throughout Punjab, one gets an idea of the enormous extent of killing taking place in Police hands. Inderjit Singh Jaijee reminds us of the urgency of the situation when he says, "It is difficult to arrive at the exact number of lives lost because of the illegal nature of the killings and the deliberate disinformation spread by the government about the number killed."[238] Workers confirm that most of these bodies had their hands and feet tied together. Although the bodies had been too mutilated by the water for any signs of torture to be seen, a majority of the bodies were found downstream of interrogation centers. Human rights workers and the people of Punjab alike believe that several of these bodies are those of the disappeared.

The utter size of the Punjab Police and supplementary army forces is an interesting point to consider. The number of officers from Punjab itself, supplemented by battalions from UP, Madhya Pradesh, Rajasthan, Gujrat, and Andhra Pradesh, in addition to paramilitary forces, exceeded six hundred thousand.[239] With about three million Sikhs between the ages of 15 and 60 in Punjab[240], that amounts to one police or paramilitary person for about five Sikh men and women. Was a police and paramilitary force of six hundred thousand needed to keep the Sikh population of Punjab in check? It is much more likely that this many men and troops were needed for intimidation, torture and extrajudicial and custodial killings that had sadly, become a part of everyday life for the Sikhs. On September 16th, 1994, the Supreme Court itself admitted that they were, "deeply concerned about the safety of the citizenry at the hands of such an errant high-handed and unchecked police force."[241]

Although a Police Raj or kingdom has existed in Punjab since Indira Gandhi came to power, it is clear that the police functions in conjunction with the central government; or rather, that they work *for* the central government. While it could not be more obvious that the Punjab Police is an "errant high-handed and unchecked police force," the covert methods of the Indian government allow it to exist as an errant and unchecked police force as well. Before resigning on May 31st, 1990, Governor Nirmal Mukarji told the *Times of India* correspondent that, "the brunt of the police raaj was being felt by the Sikh masses who had no place to go for redressal of their grievances."[242] Later, in 1991, a report published in *The Tribune* on September 5 stated, "Although the police is openly resorting to the illegal arrest of released militants, neither the Punjab and Haryana High Court nor the Sessions Judge has power to give directions to the police to stop this."[243] When appeals to the government at the local, state and national level are given no recognition, then how can one expect a father, a mother or an entire village not to raise their voice in protest. Government oppression and negligence of such magnitude is not acceptable. The machinations of the Indian government are clear: first incite rebellion by brutally slaughtering thousands of innocents, and then punish those that rebel by torture, extortion, and more genocide. Retired Justice Ajit Singh Bains wrote in 1992[244]:

Armed struggle by large or small sections of the people against governments which are either colonial or totalitarian in essence, or oblivious to the desires and wishes of the populace, cannot be included in the definition of terrorism. When every recourse to justice is exhausted, the people are compelled to take the road of armed struggle and this measure is applauded and broadly supported. Armed struggle is nothing new and there are so many such struggles recorded in modern history, from the American War of Independence in 1776 and the French Revolution in 1789 to the anti-fascist world war of liberation and the struggle of the Vietnamese and Indochinese people and others since then. To equate this means of liberation with terrorism will not hold...Terrorism, strictly speaking, is an act of intimidation of innocent people, threatening their lives, destroying their property, depriving them of their liberty and creating tension amongst them...It is to sabotage a just struggle and make the people vulnerable to the attacks of the state...The struggle of the people of South Africa against the racist regime cannot be called a terrorist movement...if a state gives rise to a cult of violence and replaces democratic means with dictatorship, it is universally recognized that people have no other recourse.

The parliamentary system in India is heavily structured on the pattern of the British Parliamentary system, though it is clear that in India, this system does not function properly. This is not due to a flaw in the parliamentary system, but rather to the actual application and implementation of the laws, or lack thereof, in India. Whereas in Britain, Canada and other commonwealth countries the parliamentary system works quite well, in India it malfunctions because of corruption of the politicians. It is essentially the Prime Minister who controls all affairs in India, and when the Prime Minister of the country falls to corruption, so does the government.

It is commonly said that the media is the fourth branch of the government, because it provides an additional system of checks and balances on the other three governmental branches. Although in a real democracy one would expect the media to be separated and independent from politics, in the case of India, we would be naive to hold such expectations.

The credibility of the media is derived from its independent and unbiased nature. Yet in India, as journalists and reporters are overtly controlled by the legislative branch headed by the Prime Minister[245], media has lost the little integrity that it began with.

Due to the heavy government censorship and surveillance of broadcast and print media, the horrific mass-scale genocide taking place all over India has been kept very well concealed by the government.[246] During several emergency situations, and especially during Operation Bluestar, Operation Woodrose, Operation Rakshak, and throughout the Emergency days and President's Rule, large blank white spaces would appear in nationally printed newspapers.[247] These spaces would indicate the missing stories of those that were killed by the police and army or the stories that touched even slightly upon the machinations of the government. The editors of newspapers would be forced to hand over the finalized versions of the paper to government inspectors who would prohibit the publication of certain articles that gave any sympathy to the oppressed communities or that shed a black light on the ruling party. Since this would not allow enough time for journalists to replace these stories, large white spaces could be found scattered throughout newspapers and even on the front page. Other newspapers left large empty white spaces in protest to the government's censorship of the media.[248]

Further, the so-called "buying" of important journalists throughout India indicated the heavy government control and infiltration in the media. The journalists that cooperated with the government and published articles that served their goals were rewarded with lavish cars, money, and other gifts of appreciation. In fact, almost all journalists residing in Chandigarh lived in houses that were specially made for government employees. Within a few years, this mass corruption of the media was so prevalent and commonplace that it ceased to be shocking.[249]

Proof of the government surveillance and badgering of innocents and journalists is given in the circular labeled "Top Secret," given from the Home Secretary to all agencies and the Department of Posts and Telegraphs on May 25th, 1994. This circular authorized the censorship of mail, telegraphs, and phone calls of certain organizations and journalists including the Akali Dal, Dal Khalsa, All India Sikh Students Federation, Sikh Lawyers Forum and several other independent and private Sikh organizations.[250]

For their effort and success in controlling the media, we must commend the politicians and policemen, for very few stories of the innocents that were targeted passed the preliminary stages of publishing. In addition to obliterating vital news from the media, these very politicians fought hard to manipulate stories to gain public support for pogroms. An example of how circumstances were given this interesting twist to favor the police aggression and violence appeared in the *Times of India* on August 4th, 1984. One of the front-page headlines screamed, "Two Sikhs hijack bus, kidnap boy." The story is as follows: two men, one wearing a turban, one clean-shaven, hijacked a bus and kidnapped a boy who was a Sikh. It was revealed later that a servant that had been dismissed by the family had kidnapped the boy for ransom. As Pritam Singh analyzed in *Punjab in Indian Politics*, the headline could have easily read, "School bus hijacked, Sikh child kidnapped."[251] Clearly, one version portrays the Sikhs as the aggressor who will not spare even children, while the other portrays the Sikhs as the helpless victim of violence. Hardly through omission, such inflammatory propaganda littered broadcast and print media, changing public opinion and intentionally forcing communal hatred and enmity to evolve. The evident discrimination poisoned not only the minds of the trusting Hindus who were lead to believe that their Sikh brothers were dangerous, but also the helpless Sikhs who knew that they had done no wrong.

The lawlessness of the police, the methods used to torture and murder, and the politician's involvement in the crimes taking place in India, remain largely hidden from the public eye. Many people believe that information they gather from newspapers, radio stations and television must be true. What they do not realize is that the Government of India does not tell the truth, it tells the *selective* truth and even that is generally mutilated.

Although many laws and regulations exist, hardly any are implemented, leaving the Indian Parliamentary system virtually ineffective. Congressmen refuse to honor the constitution, judges incessantly ignore legislation, and policemen pay no heed to the law. One clear example of this is Section 167 of India's Code of Criminal Procedure, which states that the arrested must be produced before a magistrate within twenty-four hours. It is a rare man indeed, that finds himself in front of a magistrate at all, much less within twenty-four hours. As retired Justice Ajit Singh Bains wrote in 1992 from his cell in Chandigarh's Burail jail where he was being held, "In the hands of unscrupulous people, even the most democratic and humane state can become oppressive, tyrannical and dictatorial. In such cases, the rule of law is the casualty."[252] With congressmen, judges, and police officers disobeying laws, it is in fact a group of heartless, merciless criminals that dominate India's politics.

CHAPTER 10
The Struggle for Justice

...It is a terrible tale, carefully documented, of sadistic torture, ruthless killings, fake encounters, calculated ill-treatment of women and children, and corruption and graft on a large scale...

Justice V.M. Tarkunde[253]

Documented here is the story of the Sikh community in India that was oppressed first through the army action in Punjab on the Harmandir Sahib, and then with the earthquake of organized attacks that shook the country as a whole. As the Citizens of Democracy report so insightfully states, it is indeed, "one of the most gory and tragic chapters in the entire history of modern India."[254] After the brutal attack on the Sikhs' most prominent gurduara in 1984, over 250,000 Sikhs have been murdered in India, the official number as presented by the Punjab State Magistracy[255] as well as the United States House of Representatives.[256] Since 1984, the life of a Sikh in India has not been the same. Today, the merciless attacks on the Sikhs continue. International awareness of the draconian laws and unjustified genocide is the only hope of survival for the thousands of defenseless victims in Punjab. Sadly, the brutalities, killings, desecration and destruction by the Indian government and Punjab Police remain unheard by most of the international community.

Thousands of innocent Sikhs continue to be detained in prisons for alleged acts of violence that they have never committed, and as a police officer himself admitted, are not even *capable* of committing[257]:

> *The number of cases had been intentionally increased by creating false cases, in order to justify the existence of Special Courts and N.S.A. [National Security Act] As the trial takes a very long time, generally the accused, though innocent, 'confess' the guilt in the hope of quick release.*

They rot in prison while their cases are forgotten over the years. But they are the lucky ones. The ill-fated Sikhs that are captured by the police suffer inhumane torture and excruciatingly painful deaths. The families of these victims, having no source of income, are forced into poverty. They have committed no crime, save remaining devout followers of their religion. Yet on February 15th, 2000, the United Nations declared in their Position Paper on India that:

> *India totally adheres to the Universal Declaration of Human Rights both in letter and spirit. India has in place an active National Commission for Human Rights and its judicial system too is sensitive to this issue. India allows access to various International Human Rights Organizations...India believes that torture and terrorism, especially if undertaken by those responsible for protecting the people, are a gross violation of human rights and treats them as such.*

The utter inaccuracy of this statement leaves us dumbfounded, questioning whether we are speaking of the same country at all. Even the Attorney General of India, Soli Sorabjee, admitted to the fact that human rights agencies such as Amnesty International are still barred from entering areas in Punjab.[258] Neither the judicial system nor the NHRC have made any significant attempt to punish those responsible for the grave human rights violations, nor have they provided redress to the majority of victims.

Further, violations of the *Universal Declaration of Human Rights* and other human rights abuses continue in India to this day. Families of victims are threatened and do not file complaints against officials out of fear for their lives. Hundreds of young Sikh boys are abducted by the police force every year, never to be returned to their loved ones. They are taken to torture chambers where they suffer the most inhumane abuses, eventually to be shot by the very institution that was created for their protection. Still, this is not all. Their bodies are not returned to their families, because they are too disfigured and crippled to be taken out in public. Rather, the corpses are thrown into the irrigation canals of Punjab where they float away as name-less pieces of flesh, or they are taken at night to crematoriums to be burned in mass cremations, where the evidence of their torture will reach the outside world only as ashes. Their families remain unaware of if their sons and fathers are still in jail or if they are dead. No con-firmation of death is given by the police, who either claim that the man was never in their custody, or simply that he ran away to Pakistan to promote the supposed separatist insurgency. Those that file complaints or seek redress are labeled as terrorists, separatists and extremists, and the same harsh treatment is meted out to them, regardless of their gender or their age. The Citizens for Democracy report tells of a villager who claims[259]:

> *Police is terrorising the people. All those who are to protect us, like B.S.F.[Border Security Force], Punjab Police, C.R.P.[Central Reserve Police], military and Central Government forces are the real terrorists and extremists; because terrorists are those who have crossed all limits of law and humanity.*

The cries of the tortured and abused in Punjab have fallen on deaf ears. The international community has neglected to recognize these violations, and has failed to take any action against the Indian government to prevent such atrocities in the future. Thus, India continues on this violent path of religious cleansing, never to be stopped or placed in check by any outside force. Thousands more will disappear.

Justice V. M. Tarkunde stated in his Foreword to *Oppression In Punjab*, why the truth about Operation Bluestar and the subsequent events is crucial information for all people, especially leaders of democratic countries[260]:

> *This is necessary not only for understanding the present situation in Punjab, but also in order that we should appreciate what happens when democratic rule is allowed to be replaced by a rule of the army and the police. The recent events in Punjab present an object lesson of how a democratic polity should not deal with a situation of acute public unrest.*

> *In a democracy, public unrest must be met by democratic means...Law and order have to be maintained, but they must be maintained by just and fair laws. Terrorism must be eliminated, but that should be done by taking public into confidence and isolating the terrorists from the bulk of the people. Justice and fair play must characterise the approach of a democratic government on all occasions of public unrest.*

Today, in the 21st century, we must stand up in the face of oppression and protect the innocent people who are incapable of protecting themselves. It is our duty as human beings to ensure that the right to life of *all* persons, regardless of their age, religion and gender is upheld. If it is a government that is particularly tyrannical, then we must call attention to this unjust rule. A government where the justice system is non-existent, human rights violations occur by authorities without any punishment or consequence, and hundreds of thousands of innocents die through torture by the police, is in essence, no government at all. In August of 1999, United States Congressman Dana Rohrabacher stated that for minorities such as Sikhs and Kashmiri Muslims, "India might as well be Nazi Germany."[261]

On February 28th, 2002, 42 members of the United States Congress wrote to President George W. Bush to request India to free the prisoners that are still being held hostage in their own country. They stated:

A report published last year by the Movement Against State Repression (MASR) showed that the Indian Government admitted that it held 52,268 Sikhs as political prisoners. These prisoners are being held without charges and without trials under the repressive law called TADA which expired six years ago. Some have been held since 1984, a duration of 18 years. In addition, Amnesty International reports that tens of thousands of Christians, Muslims, and other minorities are also being held as political prisoners. This is occurring while India proclaims itself "the world's largest democracy." Political prisoners are unacceptable in any country, but especially in one that proclaims democratic values.

The fanatic Hindu groups of India control the government as well as the Hindu masses – they brainwash and they manipulate. There is no doubt that they wholeheartedly believe that minorities do not exist in India; that these Sikhs, Muslims, Jains, Christians and Jews are only misguided and confused. They make it their goal to eradicate the confusion. Take Bal Thackeray, a member of the fanatic Hindu group Shiv Sena, for example, who when questioned as to whether "the Muslims were beginning to feel like the Jews in Nazi Germany said that if they behaved like Jews in Nazi Germany, then there is nothing wrong if they are treated as Jews were in Nazi Germany."[262]

The evidence of foul play in India is given through the recent murder of 35 Sikhs in Kashmir in 2001. India's national security advisor was quick to blame the massacre on Hizbul Mujahiddin and Lashkar-e-Toiba guerrillas, two of the major fanatical pro-Pakistani organizations. He spoke of the "ethnic cleansing" by Muslim guerrillas, while people neglected to notice the persistent denials from both organizations, which are typically eager to claim credit for acts of violence that they commit in the name of Islam. Yet Barry Bearak of the New York Times saw through the transparency of the Indian government's victimizing of itself. He recognized the deceptiveness He recognized that the purpose of these attacks, most probably staged by the government itself, was to influence westerners into taking harsher action against Pakistan in this time of nuclear-power uncertainty. There was little reason, it seemed, for the guerrillas to kill Sikhs, a community they had never targeted before, just prior to President Bill Clinton's visit; such action would clearly discredit their cause.[263]

Let us not fall into this illusion that all is well in India, where our brothers and sisters are slaughtered for their religious beliefs. Let us not tolerate the grave human rights abuses that occur in over fifty countries across the world for the purpose of ethnic and religious cleansing. For as we shut our eyes to these atrocities and ignore the anguished cries of the millions upon millions of our fellow human beings, we silently acquiesce to the inhumane crimes that are taking place. How then, can we say that we are any better than the evil forces that are committing such heinous crimes? Only by acknowledging past atrocities can we be sure that our children, our children's children, and *their* children, will not one day fall prey to such grave abuses in the future.

> *Violence which destroys homes and buildings is serious, but violence directed against the dignity of the individual is intolerable and unworthy of man. ...if we remain silent, the clamor of violence will stifle the cry of the people, who call for justice and peace.*[264]

Notes

1   Ram Narayan Kumar (Committee for Coordination on Disappearances in Punjab) and Dr. Cynthia Mahmood (University of Notre Dame, USA). *Disappearances in Punjab and the Impunity of the Indian State: A Report On Current Human Rights Efforts.* 1 Oct, 1998. **http://www.panthkhalsa.org/humanrights/**

2   Justice V. R. Krishna Iyer. Cited in: *Genesis of Communal Violence in India.* **http://www.panjab.org.uk/english/genesis.html**

3   UN Secretary General, at the ceremony for the submission of the report of the Historical Clarification Commission of Guatemala, in Guatemala City, February 25, 1999.

4   The literal translation of kirpan means grace. The kirpan is a small sword symbolizing freedom from oppression and injustice, and the protection of all mankind from tyranny.

5   Inderjit S. Jaijee. POLITICS OF GENOCIDE: PUNJAB 1984-1994. Chandigarh: Baba Publishers, 1995, p. 12.

6   Gurtej Singh. *Torture to Make Medieval Mughals Look Humane.* CHAKRAVYUH – WEB OF INDIAN SECULARISM. Institute of Sikh Studies, Chandigarh. 2000. pp. 120-123.

7   Dr. I. J. Singh and G. Kaur. *Resource for Future Historians.* **http://www.sikhe.com/gsdno/articles/ajune2001/06042001/resourceforfuturehistorians.htm**

8   *Amnesty International. India: A vital opportunity to end impunity in Punjab.* AI Index: ASA 20/024/1999 **http://web.amnesty.org/library/index/ENGASA200241999** 1 August, 1999.

9   Soli J. Sorabjee, former Attorney General of India. *Judicial Protection of Human Rights.* Lecture at Cornell Law School, Cornell University, Ithaca, New York. October 2nd, 2003.

10 Citizens for Democracy: OPPRESSION IN PUNJAB. Hind Mazdoor Kisan Panchayat, Delhi. 1985. p. 18.

11 United Nations' Position Paper on India. February 15th, 2000. **http://www.unol.org/pospapers/ppindia.html**

12 Dr. I. J. Singh. *1984 Revisited.* May 21, 2001. **http://www.sikhe.com/gsdno/articles/amay2001/05222001/1984revisited.htm**

13 M. K. Gandhi. COMMUNAL UNITY. Navjivan, Ahmedabad, 1948. pp. 165-167. Iqbal Singh. THE PUNJAB CRISIS AND HUMAN RIGHTS. Chicago: Citizens for Human Rights and Civil Liberties, 1985, p. 51.

[14] Citizens for Democracy. Forward to the U.S. edition, pp. 2-3.

[15] Kapur Singh. *Betrayal of the Sikhs*. Address to the Indian parliament, September 6, 1966. **http://www.sikh-history.com/sikhhist/archivedf/feature-oct2000.html**

[16] Inderjit S. Jaijee, p. 5.

[17] THE STATESMAN, Calcutta. July 7, 1946.
Justice Ajit Singh Bains. Siege of the Sikhs: Violations of Human Rights in Punjab. The New Magazine Publishing Co. Ltd. Toronto, Canada. 1988. p. 108.

[18] Inderjit S. Jaijee, p. 3.

[19] Kapur Singh. SAACHI SAKHI. 1972. p. 107 as cited in Sangat Singh. THE SIKHS IN HISTORY. Uncommon Books.New Delhi. 1999. p. 257.

[20] David Crystal: *Languages*. CIVILIZATION, February-March 1997, p. 44.

[21] Dr. Ranbir S. Sandhu STRUGGLE FOR JUSTICE. Dublin: Sikh Educational and Religious Foundation, 1999, p. xiii.

[22] Kuldip Nayar and Khushwant Singh. TRAGEDY OF PUNJAB, Vision Books, New Delhi, 1984, p. 69.

[23] Inderjit S. Jaijee, p. 7.

[24] ibid, p. 3.

[25] ibid, p. 4.

[26] H. S. Mattewal. *SYL: Only Fresh Adjudication Can Save Punjab's Case*. THE TRIBUNE – ONLINE EDITION. 25 November, 2002.
http://www.tribuneindia.com/2002/20021125/agro.htm

[27] Letter from Committee for Coordination on Disappearances in Punjab to the Ambassador of the United States in India. March 22, 2000. Sent from Chandigarh to New Delhi.

[28] The Akali Dal is the political party of the Sikhs.

[29] The Nirankaris, or Sant Nirankaris are a cult that follow a living human guru, as opposed to Guru Granth Sahib. Gurbachan Singh was the Guru during the time of this conflict.

[30] This reformist group was started in the second half of the nineteenth century by Swami Dayanand.

[31] This is the day when Khalsa, or brotherhood of Sikhs, had been established in 1699. The significance of this date within the Sikh population can be equated with the joy and excitement that surrounds Christmas for Christians.

[32] An organization of religiously devout Sikhs

[33] Kapur Singh. THEY MASSACRE SIKHS, A White Paper produced by the Shiromani Gurduara Prabandhak Committee, India, in May of 1978.

[34] Dr. Ranbir S. Sandhu, p. vi.

[35] Kuldip Nayar and Khushwant Singh, p. 9.

[36] Dr. Ranbir S. Sandhu, p. v-vi.

[37] Holding the office of Chief Minister in India is similar to holding the office of Governor in the United States.

[38] Dr. Ranbir S. Sandhu, p. xxix.

[39] ibid, p. 112.

[40] William Stevens. *Punjab Raid: Unanswered Questions*. The New York Times. June 19, 1984.

[41] S. M. Sathananthan, Dr. K. T. Lalvani, S. Raghunath Iyengar, Prof. G. P. Mansukhani, Asha Bhatnagar, Prof. V. S. Godbole (Poona), Hukum Singh. *Hindu Sikh Conflict in Punjab, Causes and Cure.* TRANSATLANTIC INDIA TIMES. 1983. **http://www.maboli.com/Sikh_HR/pages/background.htmld/peaceful.html**

[42] Citizens for Democracy. Foreword to the U.S. edition, p. 3.

[43] Amritdhari: one who has been formally initiated into the religion.

[44] Citizens for Democracy, p. 10.

[45] Dr. Ranbir S. Sandhu, p. xxvii.

[46] ibid, p. xxix.

[47] Iqbal Singh, p. 8.

Dr. Ranbir S. Sandhu, p. xxvii.

[48] INDIA TODAY. 31 December, 1983, p. 36.

[49] Citizens for Democracy, p. 17.

[50] President's Rule is allowed for under Article 356 of the Indian Constitution. It provides for the national government to dissolve the state government and leave it in the hands of the President. Essentially, it eliminates any political structure and elections, making the state a dictatorship rather than a democracy.

[51] Human Rights Watch/Asia and Physicians for Human Rights. DEAD SILENCE: THE LEGACY OF ABUSES IN PUNJAB. Publisher: Human Rights Watch, New York, 1994, p. 10.

[52] Ram Narayan Kumar and Georg Sieberer. THE SIKH STRUGGLE. Delhi: Chanakya Publications, 1991, p. 265-266.

[53] Sikh religious place of worship.

[54] Government of India: WHITE PAPER ON THE PUNJAB AGITATION. New Delhi: Government of India Press, 1984, p. 44.

[55] Citizens for Democracy, p. 53.

[56] ibid, Foreword to the U.S. edition, p. 1.

[57] Inderjit S. Jaijee, p. 262.

[58] Citizens for Democracy, p. 53.

[59] ibid, p. 56.

[60] WHITE PAPER ON THE PUNJAB AGITATION, p. 48.

[61] Citizens for Democracy, p. 57.

[62] ibid, p. 57.

[63] The only radio station in India at the time. The All India Radio was run by the Indian Government.

[64] Citizens for Democracy, p. 57.

[65] ibid, p. 58.

[66] ibid, p. 59.

[67] Mary Anne Weaver. *India reels as siege of Sikhs' holiest shrine comes to an end.* CHRISTIAN SCIENCE MONITOR, 8 June, 1984.

[68] The marble perimeter of the Harmandir Sahib.

[69] Citizens for Democracy, pp. 59-60.

[70] ibid, p. 63.

[71] WHITE PAPER ON THE PUNJAB AGITATION, pp. 47-48.

[72] Citizens for Democracy, p. 61.

[73] WHITE PAPER ON THE PUNJAB AGITATION, p. 51.

[74] Citizens for Democracy, p. 63.

[75] ibid, p. 63.

[76] Ram Narayan Kumar and Georg Sieberer, p. 265.

[77] Inderjit S. Jaijee, p. 29.

[78] Carl W. Ernst. FOLLOWING MUHAMMAD: RETHINKING ISLAM IN THE CONTEMPORARY WORLD. Chapel Hill: The University of North Carolina Press, 2003, p. 123.

[79] Cynthia K. Mahmood *Writing the Bones*. HUMAN RIGHTS REVIEW. 1999, Vol. 1, p. 28.

[80] Citizens for Democracy, pp. 53-74.

[81] The Sikh Network. SIKHISM AND THE SIKH PEOPLE – A REFERENCE GUIDE. p. 5-3.

[82] Joyce Pettigrew. THE SIKHS OF THE PUNJAB: UNHEARD VOICES OF STATE AND GUERRILLA VIOLENCE, Zed Books Ltd., London, U.K. 1995, p. 8.

[83] Citizens for Democracy, pp. 8-9.

[84] WHITE PAPER ON THE PUNJAB AGITATION, p. 169.

[85] Inderjit S. Jaijee, pp. 29-30.

[86] Joyce Pettigrew. *Take Not Arms Against Thy Sovereign*. SOUTH ASIA RESEARCH, UK, Vol 4, No 2, November 1984, pp. 116-117.

[87] Gurpurabs are days related to significant events in Sikh history.

[88] Citizens for Democracy, p. 61.

[89] Mary Anne Weaver. *India reels as siege of Sikhs' holiest shrine comes to an end.* CHRISTIAN SCIENCE MONITOR, 8 June, 1984.

[90] Soli J. Sorabjee. *Judicial Protection of Human Rights.* Human Rights organizations have been prevented from entering Punjab and other disturbed areas since 1979. THE SIKH NETWORK. SIKHISM & THE SIKH PEOPLE. A REFERENCE GUIDE. Sikh Network, 2002, p. 5-1.

[91] India became a signatory of the ICCPR on April 10th 1979.

[92] International Covenant on Civil and Political Rights, U.N. General Assembly Resolution 2200 A(XXI) of 16 December 1966.

[93] Citizens for Democracy, p. 61.

[94] WHITE PAPER ON THE PUNJAB AGITATION, pp. 47, 51, 169-170.

[95] Citizens for Democracy, p. 74.

[96] THE ECONOMIST, July 14, 1984.

[97] Iqbal Singh, p. 6.

[98] Ralph Singh, Barbara Joshi, and Surjit Singh, eds. THE TURNING POINT: INDIA'S FUTURE DIRECTION? Syracuse: Committee on Human Rights, 1985, p. 17.

[99] Ajoy Bose. *The Legacy of Fear*. THE MANCHESTER GUARDIAN. July 1, 1984.

[100] Manohar S. Batra MEMOIRS OF GIANI ZAIL SINGH: THE SEVENTH PRESIDENT OF INDIA. New Delhi: Har-Anand Publications Pvt. Ltd., 1997, p. 179.

[101] WHITE PAPER ON THE PUNJAB AGITATION, pp. 57-58.

[102] ibid, p. 55.

[103] An organization that manages the historic gurduaras in the country.

[104] WHITE PAPER ON THE PUNJAB AGITATION, p. 26.

[105] Dr. Subramanian Swamy. *In the Theater of Violence*. THE ILLUSTRATED WEEKLY OF INDIA. May 13, 1984, p. 10.

[106] ibid, p. 10.

[107] Iqbal Singh, p. 12.

[108] Ralph Singh, p. 17.

[109] WHITE PAPER ON THE PUNJAB AGITATION, p. 45, p. 48.

[110] MEMOIRS OF GIANI ZAIL SINGH: THE SEVENTH PRESIDENT OF INDIA. p. 178.

[111] WHITE PAPER ON THE PUNJAB AGITATION, p. 49.

[112] Citizens for Democracy, p. 63.

[113] The right to life, liberty and security of person is guaranteed under Article 3 of the Indian Constitution.

[114] WHITE PAPER ON THE PUNJAB AGITATION, p. 49.

[115] ibid, p. 50.

[116] MEMOIRS OF GIANI ZAIL SINGH: THE SEVENTH PRESIDENT OF INDIA. p. 183.

[117] Citizens for Democracy, p. 67.

[118] WHITE PAPER ON THE PUNJAB AGITATION, p. 44.

[119] ibid, p. 48.

[120] Citizens for Democracy, pp. 66-67.

[121] A lakh is the equivalent of one hundred thousand.

[122] WHITE PAPER ON THE PUNJAB AGITATION, p. 50.

[123] Ralph Singh, pp. 26, 67 and 69.

[124] Ram Narayan Kumar and Georg Sieberer, p. 265.

[125] Gobind Thukral. INDIA TODAY. September 30, 1984, p. 25.

[126] WHITE PAPER ON THE PUNJAB AGITATION, pp. 44-45.

[127] Ralph Singh, p. 19, 20, 21.

[128] The Guru Granth Sahib is the holy book of the Sikhs as compared to the Jewish Torah and the Christian Bible.

[129] INDIA TODAY. July 31, 1984, p. 27-29.

[130] Ram Narayan Kumar and Georg Sieberer, pp. 265-266.

[131] Ralph Singh, p. 17.

[132] Citizens for Democracy, pp. 10-11.

[133] MEMOIRS OF GIANI ZAIL SINGH: THE SEVENTH PRESIDENT OF INDIA. pp. 179-180.

[134] Iqbal Singh, p. ii.

[135] People's Union for Democratic Rights (PUDR) and People's Union for Civil Liberties (PUCL). WHO ARE THE GUILTY? Report of a joint inquiry into the causes and impact of the riots in Delhi from 31 October to 10 November 1984. Delhi: Sunny Graphics, 1984, p. 1.

[136] MEMOIRS OF GIANI ZAIL SINGH: THE SEVENTH PRESIDENT OF INDIA. p. 209-210.

[137] Mary Anne Weaver. *Post-assassination violence against Sikhs in India was allegedly planned.* CHRISTIAN SCIENCE MONITOR, 15 November, 1984.

[138] Inderjit S. Jaijee, p. 31.

[139] ibid, pp. 2-11.

[140] WHITE PAPER ON THE PUNJAB AGITATION, p. 44.

[141] William Claiborne. THE WASHINGTON POST. November 6, 1984.

[142] WHO ARE THE GUILTY?, pp. 1-2.

[143] ibid, p. 15.

[144] ibid, pp. 4 and 5.

[145] ibid, p. 4.

[146] S.M. Sikri, Chief Justice of India (Retired), et al, REPORT OF THE CITIZENS' COMMISSION. Delhi: Tata Press, 1985, p. 17.

[147] WHO ARE THE GUILTY?, p. 2

[148] MEMOIRS OF GIANI ZAIL SINGH: THE SEVENTH PRESIDENT OF INDIA. pp. 207-208.

[149] WHO ARE THE GUILTY?, p. 2.
MEMOIRS OF GIANI ZAIL SINGH: THE SEVENTH PRESIDENT OF INDIA. p. 209.

[150] MEMOIRS OF GIANI ZAIL SINGH: THE SEVENTH PRESIDENT OF INDIA. p. 209-210.

[151] ibid, p. 210.

[152] Justice V.M. Tarkunde. TRUTH ABOUT DELHI VIOLENCE. Citizens for Democracy. Delhi. 1985. p. 17.

[153] WHO ARE THE GUILTY?, pp. 6 and 8.

[154] Doordarshan is a government run national television station.

[155] Inderjit S. Jaijee, p. 230.

[156] MEMOIRS OF GIANI ZAIL SINGH: THE SEVENTH PRESIDENT OF INDIA. p. 212.

[157] WHO ARE THE GUILTY?, p. 9.

[158] ibid, p. 9.

[159] ibid, pp. 5 and 10.

[160] William Stevens. *Gandhi tells throng bullets will not shake India.* THE NEW YORK TIMES. Nov. 20, 1984.

[161] Inderjit S. Jaijee, p. 30.

[162] Tavleen Singh. *To Revive the Cong, Sonia Needs to Kill Its Sycophancy Culture.* INDIA TODAY. March 30, 1998.

[163] Mary Anne Weaver. *Post-assassination violence against Sikhs in India was allegedly planned.* CHRISTIAN SCIENCE MONITOR, 15 November, 1984.

[164] Inderjit S. Jaijee, pp. 31 & 33.

[165] Dr. Amitav Ghosh. *The Ghost of Indira Gandhi.* THE NEW YORKER. July 17, 1995.

[166] TRUTH ABOUT DELHI VIOLENCE. Chapter 5.

[167] MEMOIRS OF GIANI ZAIL SINGH: THE SEVENTH PRESIDENT OF INDIA. p. 214.

[168] Amnesty International. *Memorandum to the Government of India.* http://www.amnestyusa.org/countries/india/document.do?id=40DBAFFFFF962E7F802569A600604FFD

[169] Dr. Ranbir S. Sandhu, p. x.

[170] An FIR, or First Information Report is filed as soon as possible after a crime. It is the police record of the witness' complaint, and is pivotal for keeping records, as well as for compensation and redress.

[171] Citizens for Democracy, p. 29.

[172] Amnesty International. *India – Deaths in Custody in 1993.* May 31, 1994 http://www.amnestyusa.org/countries/india/document.do?id=6E0FA25009332641802569A600604F96

[173] Citizens for Democracy, p. 47.

[174] See reference 2.

[175] The kirpan is a small sword symbolizing the freedom from oppression and tyranny of Sikhs and non-Sikhs alike.

[176] Judge J. Painter. Verdict on Appeal No. C-950777 Court of Appeals of Ohio, First Appelate District, Hamilton County.

[177] BAAT CHEET, Indian Army Bulletin, Government of India. Serial Number 153, June 1984; reproduced in Surya Monthly, October 1984, p. 6.

[178] Ghotna: place a heavy log of wood behind the knees and stretch the heels towards the back, pressing all nerves and muscles to the point of rupture.

[179] Belna: place a long piece of wood on the thighs and have two heavy officers stand on the ends of the log and roll it.

[180] Inderjit S. Jaijee, p. 115.

[181] ibid, p. 123-124.

[182] Dr. Ranbir S. Sandhu, p. 34.

[183] Here, torture was defined as:
Any act by which severe pain or suffering, whether physical or mental, is intentionally inflicted by or at the instigation of a public official on a person for such purposes as obtaining from him or a third person information or confession, punishing him for an act he has committed or is suspected of having committed, or intimidating him or other persons.

[184] Human Rights Watch/Asia and Physicians for Human Rights, p. 22.

[185] A lathi is a wooden stick.

[186] Inderjit S. Jaijee, p. 129-131.

[187] ibid, p. 242.

[188] Cynthia K. Mahmood. Writing the Bones. p. 31.

[189] Amnesty International. *India: Break the cycle of impunity and torture in Punjab*. AI Index: ASA 20/003/2003 **http://web.amnesty.org/library/index/ENGASA200032003** Jan 19th 2003.
Amnesty International. *India: A vital opportunity to end impunity in Punjab.*

[190] Mary Anne Weaver. *India's Sikhs are bitter as Army tries to weed out 'militants'.* THE CHRISTIAN SCIENCE MONITOR, 15 October, 1984.

[191] Principle 12 of the United Nations Body of Principles for the Protection of All Persons under Any Form of Detention or Imprisonment clearly states that the following should be documented concerning a prisoner: the reasons for arrest, the time of arrest and detention, the identity of law enforcement officials concerned, and information concerning the place of custody. Although the United Nations has made clear the vital importance of such information, the Punjab Police continues to disregard their suggestions on a mass scale, generally neglecting to record any of the above.

[192] Cyberspace Graveyard for Disappeared Persons. *"Disappearances" In Punjab.* **http://www.disappearances.org/mainfile.php/articles_india/26/**

[193] Ram Narayan Kumar and Cynthia Mahmood

[194] The case of Jaswant Singh Khalra is a prime example of how human rights workers disappear in India. Please see further text or refer to Amnesty International. *India: A vital opportunity to end impunity in Punjab.*

[195] Ram Narayan Kumar, Amrik Singh, Ashok Agrwaal and Jaskaran Kaur. REDUCED TO ASHES: THE INSURGENCY AND HUMAN RIGHTS IN PUNJAB. Kathmandu: South Asia Forum for Human Rights, 2003, p. 55.

[196] Ram Narayan Kumar, Amrik Singh, Ashok Agrwaal and Jaskaran Kaur, pp. 54, 56 and 58.

[197] *The Punjab Police Rules 1934*, Chapter XXV, Rule 25.38

[198] Criminal Writ Petition No. 990 of 1995, Punjab and Haryana High Court.

[199] Meaning that the petitioner had no legal grounds to file such a petition, since the petition did not legally involve himself.

[200] Ram Narayan Kumar, Amrik Singh, Ashok Agrwaal and Jaskaran Kaur, p. 3.

[201] Amnesty International. India: *A vital opportunity to end impunity in Punjab.*

[202] Amnesty International. *A Mockery of Justice: The Case concerning the "disappearance" of human rights defender Jaswant Singh Khalra severely undermined.* AI Index: ASA 20/007/1998 **http://www.web.amnesty.org/ai.nsf/index/ASA200071998.**
Ram Narayan Kumar, Amrik Singh, Ashok Agrwaal and Jaskaran Kaur, p. 6.

[203] The CBI, or Central Bureau of Investigation, is the Indian counterpart of America's Central Intelligence Agency.

[204] Ram Narayan Kumar, Amrik Singh, Ashok Agrwaal and Jaskaran Kaur, pp. 62 and 65.

[205] ibid, p. 67.

[206] US Congressional Records, July 31, 1998. p. E1534.
THE WASHINGTON TIMES. August 4, 1998.

[207] Amnesty International. *India: A vital opportunity to end impunity in Punjab.*

[208] Article 11 of the *Principles on the Effective Prevention and Investigation of Extra-legal, Arbitrary and Summary Executions* **http://www.unhchr.ch/html/menu3/b/54.htm** states:
"In cases in which the established investigative procedures are inadequate because of lack of expertise or impartiality, because of the importance of the matter or because of the apparent existence of a pattern of abuse, and in cases where there are complaints from the family of the victim about these inadequacies or other substantial reasons, Governments shall pursue investigations through an independent commission of inquiry or similar procedure. Members of such a commission shall be chosen for their recognized impartiality, competence and independence as individuals. In particular, they shall be independent of any institution, agency or person that may be the subject of the inquiry. The commission shall have the authority to obtain all information necessary to the inquiry and shall conduct the inquiry as provided for under these Principles."

[209] Ram Narayan Kumar, Amrik Singh, Ashok Agrwaal and Jaskaran Kaur, p. 3.
The following human rights organizations and political groups came together to form the CCDP: Committee for Information and Initiative on Punjab, Punjab Human Rights Organization, Movement Against State Repression, World Human Rights Protection Council, Human Rights and Democracy Forum, Lawyers for Human Rights, Khalra Action Committee, Bhartiya Kisan Union, the three branches of the Akali Dal (Wadala, Mann, Panthik), Punjab Janata Morcha, Bahujan Samaj Party, Internationalist Democratic Party, Sikh Students Federation (Mehta/Chawla), Babbar Akali Dal, Akal Federation, and finally, the World Sikh Council (which joined later).

[210] Ram Narayan Kumar and Cynthia Mahmood

[211] Tapan Bose, Secretary-General, South Asia Forum for Human Rights, in Introduction to REDUCED TO ASHES: THE INSURGENCY AND HUMAN RIGHTS IN PUNJAB. Kathmandu: South Asia Forum for Human Rights, 2003, p. VIII.
Human Rights Watch. *India: Justice Eludes Families of the "Disappeared" in Punjab: National Human Rights Commission Should Investigate.* New York, 10 June, 2003.

[212] Amnesty International. *India: A vital opportunity to end impunity in Punjab.*

[213] Amnesty International. India: *A vital opportunity to end impunity in Punjab.*
  1) Restitution: steps should be taken to restore the victims to the situation they were in before the violation occurred, including restoration of their legal rights, social status, family life, place of residence, property and employment.

  2) Compensation: steps should be taken to compensate for any economically assessable damage resulting from violations including physical or mental harm, emotional distress, lost educational opportunities, loss of earnings, legal and/or medical costs.

  3) Rehabilitation: steps should be taken to ensure medical and psychological care if necessary as well as legal and social services.

  4) Satisfaction and guarantees of non-repetition: steps should be taken to ensure cessation of continuing violations, public disclosure of truth behind violations, official declaration of responsibility and/or apologies, public acknowledgment of violations, as well as judicial or administrative sanction, and preventive measures including Human Rights training.

[214] Amnesty International. *India: A vital opportunity to end impunity in Punjab.*

[215] ENFORCED DISAPPEARANCES, ARBITRARY EXECUTIONS AND SECRET CREMATIONS: VICTIM TESTIMONY AND INDIA'S HUMAN RIGHTS OBLIGATIONS. Interim report of the Committee for Coordination on Disappearances in Punjab, July 1999.

[216] United Nations. INTERNATIONAL COVENANT ON CIVIL AND POLITICAL RIGHTS, U. N. General Assembly Resolution 2200 A (XXI) of 16 December 1966.

[217] Office of the High Commissioner for Human Rights. DECLARATION ON THE PROTECTION OF ALL PERSONS FROM ENFORCED DISAPPEARANCES. **http://www.unhchr.ch/huridocda/huridoca.nsf/(Symbol)/A.RES.47.133.En**

[218] Amnesty International. *India: A vital opportunity to end impunity in Punjab.*

[219] Amnesty International. *India. Covering events from January – December 2002.* **http://web.amnesty.org/web/web.nsf/print/ind-summary-eng**

[220] Ram Narayan Kumar and Cynthia Mahmood

[221] Inderjit S. Jaijee, p. 61.

[222] ibid, p. 18.

[223] Justice Ajit Singh Bains was arrested on April 3rd, 1992 at 10:30 AM in Chandigarh under the TADA Legislation. **www.dalitstan.org/journal/rights/102/080492.html** THE TIMES OF INDIA. *TADA's POTOstat.* Today's Editorial. October 25, 2001. **http://timesofindia.indiatimes.com/articleshow/192911928.cms**

[224] Justice Ajit Singh Bains. *State Terrorism and Human Rights.* **http://www.cpcml.ca/tmld/TMLD222.htm**

[225] Twenty eight candidates to the elections were killed before voting could take place. Elections to a full 20% of the seats were countermanded because a candidate had met a violent death (almost all killed were Sikhs). Inderjit S. Jaijee, p. 169.

[226] STATISTICAL REPORT ON GENERAL ELECTION, 1992, TO THE LEGISLATIVE ASSEMBLY OF PUNJAB. Election Commission of India, New Delhi. 1992.

[227] Ram Narayan Kumar, Amrik Singh, Ashok Agrwaal and Jaskaran Kaur, p. 52.

[228] HINDUSTAN TIMES, November 3, 1995.

[229] Inderjit S. Jaijee, p. 61.

[230] Ram Narayan Kumar and Georg Sieberer, p. 287.

[231] Cynthia K. Mahmood. *Writing the Bones*. p. 28.

[232] Embassy of India. "The Prevention of Terrorism Ordinance." 2001
http://www.indianembassy.org/policy/Terrorism/poto_2001.htm
THE TIMES OF INDIA. *TADA's POTOstat*. Today's Editorial. October 25, 2001.
http://timesofindia.indiatimes.com/articleshow/192911928.cms
Amnesty International. "India."
http://web.amnesty.org/web/web.nsf/print/ind-summary-eng

[233] Human Rights Watch/Asia and Physicians for Human Rights. DEAD SILENCE: THE
LEGACY OF ABUSES IN PUNJAB. Publisher: Human Rights Watch, New York, 1994, p. 24.

[234] Inderjit S. Jaijee, p. 75-78.

[235] ibid, p. 53.

[236] ibid, p. 49.

[237] Ram Narayan Kumar and Cynthia Mahmood

[238] Inderjit S. Jaijee, p. 39.

[239] ibid, p. 206.

[240] ibid, p. 206-207.

[241] Tapash Chakraborty. *Mystery of the Missing Militant*.
http://www.sikhreview.org/november1994/human_rights.htm

[242] Inderjit S. Jaijee, p. 27

[243] ibid, p. 199.

[244] Justice Ajit Singh Bains. *State Terrorism and Human Rights*.
http://www.cpcml.ca/tmld/TMLD222.htm

[245] Inderjit S. Jaijee, p. 225.

[246] Iqbal Singh, pp. 16-17.
Inderjit S. Jaijee, pp. 225, 227, 231.

[247] Inderjit S. Jaijee, p. 225.

[248] ibid, p. 225.

[249] ibid, pp. 234-235.

[250] ibid, p. 239-240.

[251] ibid, p. 232-233.

[252] Justice Ajit Singh Bains. *State Terrorism and Human Rights*.
http://www.cpcml.ca/tmld/TMLD222.htm

[253] Justice V. M. Tarkunde. Foreward to 'Citizens for Democracy: *Oppression in Punjab*.'
Hind Mazdoor Kisan Panchayat, 1985, Delhi. pp. 2 and 4.

[254] Citizens for Democracy: Oppression in Punjab. Hind Mazdoor Kisan Panchayat,
Delhi. 1985.

[255] U.S. Congressman Dan Burton. "India Shows Religious 'Tolerance' By Firing on Christian Festival and Beheading A Catholic Priest." U. S. Congressional Records, 30 October, 1997, p. E2147

[256] United States Congressional Records, 19 May, 1999, p. E1031.

[257] Citizens for Democracy, p. 20.

[258] Soli J. Sorabjee. *Judicial Protection of Human Rights*.

[259] Citizens for Democracy, p. 27.

[260] Justice V. M. Tarkunde. Foreward to 'Citizens for Democracy: OPPRESSION IN PUNJAB.' Hind Mazdoor Kisan Panchayat, 1985, Delhi. pp. 2 and 4.

[261] INFOTIMES. *"Terrorist Government of India Murders Innocent People: U.S. Congressman."* **http://lists.isb.sdnpk.org/pipermail/ngo-list/2001-October/001259.html**

[262] Cynthia K. Mahmood. *Trials by Fire: Dynamics of Terror in Punjab and Kashmir.* DEATH SQUAD: THE ANTHROPOLOGY OF STATE TERROR. Jeffrey A. Sluka (editor) 2000.

[263] Amnesty International. INDIA – *A trail of unlawful killings in Jammu and Kashmir: Chithisinghpora and its aftermath* **http://web.amnesty.org/library/Index/ENGASA200242000**

[264] Pope John Paul II in Ypress, Belgium. *Pope Defends Concept of a Just War.* THE NEW YORK TIMES, 18 May, 1985.

[265] George Fernandes. *On the threshold of a fascist state*. Preface to 'Citizens for Democracy: OPPRESSION IN PUNJAB.' Hind Mazdoor Kisan Panchayat, 1985. Delhi. p. iii.

[266] One of the most influential Hindu political parties of India

[267] Suketu Mehta. *Mumbai*. GRANTA, 1997. Vol. 57, p. 120-121. Response of Mr. Thackeray, during an interview with *Time* magazine, when asked if Indian Muslims were beginning to feel like Jews in Nazi Germany.

[268] Awatar Singh Sekhon and Harjinder Singh Dilgeer. Khalistan: THE STRUGGLE TO REGAIN LOST SOVEREIGNTY. The Sikh Educational Trust, Box 60246, University of Alberta Postal Outlet, Edmonton, Alberta T6G 2S5, Canada.

[269] Cited in **http://www.panthkhalsa.org/raj/raj_khalsa.php**

[270] Awatar Singh Sekhon and Harjinder Singh Dilgeer.

The case of the government and the Congress-I is simple: Their foul deeds and criminal acts shall not be exposed. They will run wild in Punjab, killing innocent people, they will organise mass killings of Sikhs in Delhi and elsewhere; they will promote criminals in politics and in public life; they will let the police kill people without provocation. If anyone should document these brutal and criminal acts and publish the reports, such individuals or organisations that do this must be scandalised, terrorized and suppressed. This is precisely what fascism is about.

George Fernandez, former Defense Minister of India[265]

About the Author

Gunisha Kaur has been a human rights activist from the beginning of her years at Williamsville North High School, from where she graduated in 2002. It was during her studies here that she began, and completed this project on human rights violations in India. She was very active in researching human rights violations throughout her high school years, and continues on this journey even today. A preliminary version of this book has won the Joanne Champion Granger Award in 2002.

In the past few years Gunisha has focused her study on the genocide that has been taking place in India. She has been actively involved in several written works as well as presentations throughout the US and Canada that aim to educate people about these human rights violations. Currently a student at Cornell University, Gunisha has also written articles for Ik Onkar Magazine and 1984 Remembered.

"Have they behaved like the Jews in Nazi Germany? If so, there is nothing wrong if they are treated as Jews were in Nazi Germany."

Balasaheb Thackeray, founder and head of Shiv Sena[266,267]

"To preserve the unity of India, if we have to eradicate 2-kror [20 million] Sikhs, we will do so."

Balram Jakhar, Speaker of the Indian Parliament, 1980-1989[268]

"...the Indian Government has been the major cause of bloodshed in the state (Punjab)..."

New York Times, September 16th, 1985

"Indian Government is accused of inhuman barbarities against the people of Punjab."

Justice V.M. Tarkunde, Bombay High Court[269]

"A member of the Indian Government's 'Red Brigade' confessed to State-sponsored terrorism against the Sikhs."

The Ottowa Citizen, February 12th, 1989

"They put [Bagail Kaur, 7 month old] on a colony of ants, coated her arms and legs with sugar and let the ants bite away at her. They watched as she cried out helplessly as if close to death. These tyrants possess not even a grain of mercy."

U.S. Congressional Records, August 12th, 1992

"You do not know the might of armed forces. We will eliminate 5,000 Sikh youths and the world will know nothing about it."

Chandershekhar, Prime Minister of India, 1990-1991[270]